AV. 5

1 Terrina
1 Ricciolo D

1 Paccheri
1 Spaghetti D

...lellata
...nna D

il viaggio di vetri

il viaggio

il viaggio di vetri

a culinary journey

MARC VETRI WITH DAVID JOACHIM

WINE NOTES BY JEFF BENJAMIN

PHOTOGRAPHY BY DOUGLAS TAKESHI WOLFE

TEN SPEED PRESS
Berkeley | Toronto

Ten Speed Press
PO Box 7123
Berkeley, California 94707
www.tenspeed.com

Distributed in Australia by Simon and Schuster Australia, in Canada
by Ten Speed Press Canada, in New Zealand by Southern Publishers
Group, in South Africa by Real Books, and in the United Kingdom
and Europe by Publishers Group UK.

Cover and text design by Nancy Austin

On the cover, left to right: Michael Solomonov, Dionicio Jimenez,
Marc Vetri, Joey Baldino

Library of Congress Cataloging-in-Publication Data
Vetri, Marc.
  Il viaggio di Vetri : a culinary journey / Marc Vetri with
David Joachim ; wine notes by Jeff Benjamin ; photography
by Douglas Takeshi Wolfe.
     p. cm.
  Includes index.
  ISBN-13: 978-1-58008-888-6
  ISBN-10: 1-58008-888-0
  1. Cookery, Italian. 2. Vetri, Marc. I. Joachim, David. II. Title.
  TX723.V485 2008
  641.5945—dc22

                                        2008021667

Printed in China
First printing, 2008

1 2 3 4 5 6 7 8 9 10 — 12 11 10 09 08

dedica: alla bella città di "Berghem" ed a tutti gli "amis Bergamasc" che mi hanno accolto con simpatia e affetto

dedication: to the beautiful city of Bergamo and all of my "Bergamascan friends" who welcomed me with fondness and affection

CONTENTS

ACKNOWLEDGMENTS viii

FOREWORD by Piero Selvaggio xi

INTRODUCTION 1

WINE NOTES by Jeff Benjamin 3

1   THE FAMILY la famiglia 10

2   THE JOURNEY il viaggio 24

3   COLD APPETIZERS antipasti freddi 32

4   HOT APPETIZERS antipasti caldi 64

5   PASTA AND RISOTTO pasta e risotto 94

6   FISH AND SHELLFISH pesce e crostacei 152

7   MEAT carne 172

8   POULTRY, GAME, AND ORGAN MEATS 198
    pollame, selvaggina e frattaglie

9   VEGETABLE SIDE DISHES contorni 218

10 DESSERTS dolce 230

STOCKS, SAUCES, AND OTHER BASICS 270
brodo, salse e fondamentali

SOURCES 280

INDEX 283

ACKNOWLEDGMENTS

I'm a cook, not a writer. Transforming recipes into an adaptable form so that people can comprehend them and cook them is as difficult as opening a restaurant for the first time—or possibly even giving birth. It's always interesting to delve into someone else's world: it can help you understand how good you have it in your own. After steering this book through the publishing process for the past five years, I can honestly say, without hesitation, that I'm glad to be a cook! I never knew how challenging it would be to write a cookbook, or how rewarding. And I have the following people to thank:

David Joachim: If anyone can read this book and create its recipes, it is because of you. Thank you for bringing my story and recipes to life.

Jeff Benjamin: I would need another book to tell you everything you have meant to me. For now, I'll say thanks for being a voice of reason, both professionally and personally, throughout my career.

Lisa Ekus-Saffer, David Saffer, and Pebbles: Forget about the agent role. Thanks for being the best friends and mentors, and for providing great escapes.

Doug Wolfe: You are a masterful photographer and artist, and you make one helluva good cup of coffee. Thanks for capturing my food on film.

Joseph Manzare: You are the one chef/restaurateur/entrepreneur I admire the most. No one is more loyal or has more integrity. And no one appreciates you more than me.

Jeff and Claudia Michaud: Jeff, your work and persistence always push me to better myself, and Claudia is the perfect complement to you.

Ofer Shlomo: I can only say that I am the luckiest person for having met you. I'm glad you are a part of my life.

Phil Roy: Thanks for reminding me that there are still good-hearted people with no agendas out there.

Miles Angelo: Through the last twenty years, as unbelievable as it seems, you're always there to lend a hand.

The city of Bergamo and all of the people there who changed my life forever—Marco, Graziano, Massi, Ivano, Pierangelo, Alberto, Valentino, Paolo, Camillo, Luca, Peter, Stefano, and so many more: Huge hugs to you all.

Everyone at Ten Speed, especially Aaron Wehner, Nancy Austin, and Clancy Drake for guiding me through the process: I owe you a big debt of gratitude.

All the recipe testers and tasters, most of all Tara Desmond, Marilyn Anthony, Jennifer Lindner McGlinn, and Keri Fisher: Thanks for testing and re-testing until we got it right.

Brad Spence: You are the only chef de cuisine I've ever trusted enough to run Vetri, and you've been a great help with the recipes for this book.

Past and present cooks and staff at Vetri and Osteria—Michael Solomonov, Dionicio Jimenez, Joey Baldino, and everyone else who has come through my kitchen and worked so hard: I hope I've inspired you as much as you have inspired me.

Piero Selvaggio: I can't thank you enough for helping me begin my journey and trusting me to carry it through.

Grace Parisi: You are a true friend. Thanks to you and everyone else at *Food & Wine* for being so supportive of me throughout my career.

Tina Breslow: Thank you for all your help and tireless dedication from the very beginning.

The Philadelphia restaurant community: It's a pleasure to be in an industry where it's more about camaraderie than competition. Since I opened ten years ago, so many people have supported and stood by me and served as an inspiration as they work to make Philadelphia a flourishing restaurant city. Thanks especially to Georges Perrier, Jose Garces, Sal D'Angelo, Kiong Bahn, Jean Marie Lacroix, Steven Starr, Dan Stern, and Brian Sikora for always pushing the city forward. Thanks also to Philadelphia's great food purveyors, like Samuels and Sons, Wells, and Farm Art, and to farmers such as Glen Brendle, Paul at Country Time, and the farmers at Blue Moon Acres, for providing the city's chefs with such beautiful ingredients.

The French Culinary Institute, especially Alain Sailhac, Dorothy Cain Hamilton, and Alan Richman: Thank you for supporting and inspiring me ever since my days at Bella Blu.

Mom and Dad: You've always let me find my own way and helped guide me through it. You'll never know how much I appreciate it. I'll always need you.

And most important—Megan and Maurice (and Angelo): Everything that is good in my life I owe to you.

Marc Vetri, standing at right, with friends from ristorante Vissani, Italy

FOREWORD

It was in Milan, in September 1976, that I had the awakening of my life in food. You see, I was born in Sicily, raised in a typical household with Sicilian fare, and it was only in America that I was exposed to more diverse styles of food and more sophisticated restaurants. I started working in restaurants at the age of seventeen, first as a dishwasher, pizza maker, line cook, and waiter, and then as manager of a fine-dining restaurant on Sunset Boulevard in Hollywood.

When I opened Valentino in 1972, I was twenty-five and a bit "green," unaware of any other Italian cuisine than the one I was accustomed to in Italian American kitchens. My awakening came three years after opening Valentino, when I decided to travel to Italy, to the sources. Every time I sampled new dishes, I realized how much I didn't know. I finally got some better chefs at Valentino and learned more about northern Italian cuisine. I swore to make my restaurant as good as the great restaurants I had experienced in Italy. I spent most of my time in Milan and the surrounding region because I realized it was the place where the greatest local food products were combined with the greatest chefs, like Gualtiero Marchesi, Sergio Mei, Ezio Santin, and Pierangelo Cornaro. From that region, I brought to America some of the best cooking talents that have passed through our kitchens.

PREFAZIONE

Fu a Milano, nel settembre del 1976, che ebbi il risveglio della mia passione per l'arte culinaria. Sono nato in Sicilia, cresciuto in una tipica famiglia siciliana, e fu solo in America che venni esposto a diversi stili di cucina e a più sofisticati ristoranti. Iniziai a lavorare nei ristoranti all'età di diciassette anni, prima come lavapiatti, pizzaiolo, aiuto cuoco e cameriere, poi come manager di un ristorante su Sunset Boulevard a Hollywood.

Quando aprii Valentino nel 1972, avevo venticinque anni ed ero un po' «acerbo,» ignoravo l'esistenza di altre tipi di cucina italiana che non fossero quella italo-americana.

Il mio risveglio venne tre anni dopo aver aperto Valentino, quando decisi di andare in Italia, alla fonte, e assaggiando nuovi piatti, realizzai quanto poco conoscevo.

Finalmente ebbi cuochi migliori a Valentino e imparai di più della cucina del nord d'Italia. Mi promisi di far diventare il mio ristorante buono come i grandi ristoranti avevo provato in Italia. Spesi molto del mio tempo a Milano e dintorni perchè realizzai che quelli erano i posti dove la più grande produzione di prodotti locali si combinava con grandi chef come Gualtiero Marchesi, Sergio Mei, Ezio Santin e Pierangelo Cornaro.

Da quella zona, portai in America alcuni dei migliori e talentuosi cuochi siano passati dalle nostre cucine.

As Valentino grew, we established new contacts and made new friends in Italy and America. We made sure to keep up with the American scene and stayed in the forefront of the evolution of Italian food. I always sent my chefs to Italy to learn from the sources. Then, one day in 1993, a phone call came from a young chef named Marc Vetri from Philadelphia. He was living in Venice, California, and working for Wolfgang Puck. He wanted to go to Italy *per fare esperienza* (for the experience). He wanted guidance. Contacts. A starting point. I felt immediately felt great potential in this young chef, so I met with him. I heard his dream and felt his commitment. I knew quickly that he was driven, and I wrote a note about him to my group of contacts in Bergamo, from the established chefs to the up-and-coming, from the maestros to the pupils who had left me to open their own places.

Marc traveled to Bergamo and I heard back from him during his various stages, impressed with how well he had adapted to Italian culture and with his limitless desire to grow. He called me from Rome, from Piedmont, from Sicily. He kept traveling to learn from the great talents in Italy, including a top olive oil producer, a winemaker, a great *pasticciere* in Sicily, the best butcher in Panzano, an artisanal pasta maker in Tuscany, and many others.

Mentre Valentino cresceva, noi stabilemmo nuovi contatti e facemmo nuove amicizie in Italia e in America. Volevamo essere sicuri che la scena americana stesse al passo con l'evoluzione della cucina italiana. Ho sempre mandato i miei chef in Italia per imparare dalla fonte. Poi, un giorno, nel 1993, una telefonata arrivò da un giovane chef di Philadelphia, Marc Vetri. Lui viveva a Venice, in California, e lavorava per Wolfgang Puck. Marc voleva andare in Italia per fare esperienza, voleva indicazioni, contatti, un punto da dove cominciare. Sentii subito grandi potenzialità in questo giovane chef e così lo incontrai. Ascoltai i suoi sogni e sentii il suo impegno. Capii subito il suo entusiasmo e scrissi una lettera su di lui a un gruppo di miei contatti a Bergamo, da chef affermati a talenti emergenti, dai maestri ai pupilli che mi hanno lasciato per aprire il proprio ristorante.

Marc partì per Bergamo e lo risentii durante le sue varie esperienze, ero stupito di come si era adattato alla cultura italiana e di come il suo desiderio di crescere fosse senza limiti. Mi chiamò da Roma, dal Piemonte, dalla Sicilia. Marc continuò a viaggiare per imparare dai grandi talenti in Italia, inclusi un importante produttore di olio di oliva, un produttore di vino, un grande pasticciere in Sicilia, il miglior macellaio in Panzano, un artigiano della pasta in Toscana e molti altri ancora.

Marc was very serious, very focused. He lived on his savings, made friends, worked hard, proved his talent, and, in turn, was embraced as only the Italians can do. He had a plan and a dream. He was driven to open an Italian restaurant in America. Today, Marc Vetri is considered one of the finest chefs, an ambassador of Italian food in America.

A few years ago, walking through Philadelphia to Vetri for dinner, I was filled with a sense of joy, a feeling of pride, and a strong reassurance that Italian food is in the hands of Marc Vetri. He cooks true Italian food. Vetri has been the greatest stage for him to cultivate his vision and to hone his skills. And now with Osteria, we have another warm and welcoming home for hearty, traditional Italian fare. Philadelphia and the wider culinary world are richer because of Marc and his cooking.

Yet, what I like most is the path of Marc Vetri. He is a cook with a vision and a good plan. He is a hardworking realist in a world of dreamers. He wanted to learn the cooking of his family roots and bring that cooking to America. He followed his vision and returned to his hometown to make his dream a reality. We are all paid back by his cooking, his hospitality, and now also by his book. *Buon appetito!*

—Piero Selvaggio

Marc era molto serio, molto concentrato sui propri obbiettivi. Ha vissuto dei suoi risparmi, ha fatto molte amicizie , lavorato duro e dimostrato il suo talento e in cambio è stato accolto come solo gli italiani sanno fare. Marc aveva un programma e un sogno. Desiderava aprire un ristorante italiano in America. Oggi, Marc Vetri è considerato uno dei migliori chef, un ambasciatore della cucina italiana in America.

Alcuni anni fa, andando a Philadelphia per una cena a Vetri, fui preso da un senso di gioia, di orgoglio, e una forte rassicurazione che la cucina italiana fosse nelle mani di Marc Vetri. Marc cucina vero cibo italiano. Vetri è stato il posto più importante per lui, per coltivare la sua visione e affinare le sue doti. E ora, con Osteria, abbiamo un altro posto che accoglie l'autentica e tradizionale cucina italiana. Philadelphia, e il più vasto mondo culinario, sono più ricchi grazie a Marc e alla sua multi-premiata cucina.

Tuttavia, quello che più mi piace è il percorso di Marc Vetri. È uno chef con una visione e un programma. È un lavoratore realista in un mondo di sognatori. Voleva imparare la cucina delle sue origini di famiglia e portarla in America. Marc ha seguito la sua visione ed è tornato nella sua città nativa per trasformare il suo sogno in realtà. Siamo tutti stati ripagati dalla sua cucina, dalla sua ospitalità e ora anche dal suo libro. Buon appetito!

—Piero Selvaggio

INTRODUCTION

I sometimes chuckle when people talk about Vetri as one of the best Italian restaurants in the country. Don't get me wrong. It's nice to hear the praise and to be recognized. But who can say what is the best? One of my best meals was a fried rice ball I ate at a market in Sicily. I was seventeen years old, traveling with my father in his parents' hometown of Enna, in the middle of Sicily. I grew up eating *arancine* with my grandparents in South Philadelphia, but I had never tried one made by a Sicilian street vendor. At that moment, that little rice ball was the best thing I had ever put into my mouth. And who is to say I was wrong? Perception is a powerful thing. Your best meal could be an elaborate sixteen-course affair at a Michelin three-star restaurant, or a hot dog shared with someone special on a mountaintop. The best meals are more about the moment than they are about the food.

Romano Dal Forno, the Italian winemaker who revolutionized Valpolicella wine, made me understand that. In 2003, while sitting with Romano in his vineyard in Veneto, I asked him, "How long do your wines last in the bottle? How age-worthy are they?" Romano's vineyard is relatively young—about twenty years old—so to ask how long his wines will last is a little presumptuous. He just looked at me and said, "How can I tell you that? Wines last as long as they last. It is a risk. Everything is a risk. When you open a bottle of wine, it depends on everything. In France, I once opened a *premier cru Bordeaux* at a picnic with my wife, and from the moment I opened it, I could smell its incredible essence. That aroma has remained in my thoughts until this day. I can still smell and taste that bottle. Since then, I've drunk that same wine, that same vintage many times and it has never been quite the same as it was at that picnic. Maybe the wine was the same and the ambience was different. Who knows?"

Romano then looked over at my well-cut head chef, Jeff Michaud, who was sitting with his beautiful fiancée, Claudia. He turned to Claudia and said, "Look at your fiancé . . . handsome, thin, strong. What guarantees do you have that in ten years he will still look like that? What guarantees do any of us have? I've done everything I know to do to ensure that a bottle of my wine that you open in ten years will be memorable, but I cannot see into the future. I don't know under what circumstance you will be opening that wine."

Romano's response stuck with me, and I relate it to my cooking. You may like my spinach gnocchi one night and hate it the next. Like Romano, I cannot see into the future. I don't know under what circumstance you will be eating my food. I could serve you the greatest meal I have ever cooked, but you could be in a horrible mood with a lot on your mind and nothing would taste good.

If I do my job, it is a given that the food itself will be good. The real question is, will you have a great and memorable evening? I hope so. That is what I am trying to achieve. And that is why I don't just cook food at Vetri. I try to create moments—moments that will make people say, "Hey, remember that birthday meal five years ago with our friends . . . we laughed all night . . . that was at Vetri, wasn't it?" Simply put, that is the best kind of meal there is. And I am lucky—indeed, honored—that people come to my "house" to spend the most cherished moments of their lives eating my food, and then go away with a memory they can share with family and friends for years to come.

That experience is at the core of Italian cooking: a great meal shared with family and friends. It is what I learned when I first went to Italy to cook in 1993. And it is what I continue to learn every time I cook with my Italian "family" in Italy. Fresh ingredients and simple preparations are the foundations of Italian cooking, but it is people who bring a great meal to life.

WINE NOTES

vino

BY JEFF BENJAMIN

When I first became serious about wine, I cared only about French wines. I learned everything I could about Bordeaux. I could even recite the 1855 classification. I fell in love with Saint-Émilion and waxed poetic about Merlot. I was fixed on Burgundy, on Pinot Noir, and I believed that no one could make better use of Chardonnay than the French. Then I had my first Marcassin. Suddenly, I was exclaiming, "New World! Give me New World!"

In other words, I was fickle, and I didn't even know it. I simply enjoyed wine and experiencing new tastes. I learned what I could from a flock of master sommeliers, and I settled into a comfortable place with my wine knowledge—the role of good acidity, the place of strong tannins, the meaning of

Jeff Benjamin

age-worthiness, the value of viscosity. But even though I fully utilized such scholarly knowledge, I never completely embraced an academic approach to wine appreciation. Whenever I sat down to a meal, experience trumped academics, which lead to an important "Aha!" moment in my wine education. It occurred during the first of many dinners with two extraordinary wine experts.

THE JOY OF WINE

Of course, they are Italian, and Marc took me to meet them shortly after we opened Vetri in 1998. On the flight to Milan, Marc prepped me on all of the people we would be looking up: there was his confidant, Marco Rossi; his mentor-chef, Graziano Pinato; the "Boss," Pierangelo Cornaro; and many others. Then he paused and said, "You're also going to meet Alberto and Valentino. They know everything there is to know about wine. You're going to learn a lot from them." My skepticism set in. Everything? I had already met people who knew "everything."

We landed at 6:45 in the morning, picked up a rental car, and took the A4 *autostrada t*o a nearby Autogrill, a branch of Italy's popular roadside chain. Here, in the most mundane setting, we met the Italian wine distributors Valentino Rossi and Alberto Galeati for an espresso. They were speaking Italian, of which I knew very little, so I initially assumed this was their first stop in a long business day that would take them

Alberto Galeati

3

Marcello Monzio Compagnoni and Valentino Rossi

to appointments throughout northern Italy. But we spent hours talking with them, and only in the early afternoon did we go our separate ways.

Later that evening, Marc and I drove to Marco Rossi's restaurant, Le Cantine D, located above a wine store in Bergamo. All of Marc's friends from Bergamo were there, including Massi Locatelli, Valentino, Alberto, and a half dozen others. I sat next to Valentino and tried to listen in on what he was saying about wine. He was talking about Vinitaly, Italy's foremost wine trade show, where he had spent the afternoon and where Marc and I were heading the next day. But Valentino was not analyzing any particular wine. Instead, he was regaling the group with a funny thing that happened when he met with winemaker Angelo Gaja. No mention of Gaja's world-famous Barbaresco, Barolo, Brunello, or Chardonnay. No pearls of wisdom. Just a story to share among friends.

Alberto had also been at Vinitaly that afternoon. Surely, he would tell us the best wines he tasted, fill us in on who was disappointed by the vintage, let us know who scored the greatest praise. But that didn't happen. He did say that he had met a nice winemaker from Sicily named Francesca Planeta and that we should look for her the next day. He also saw an old friend who was slicing prosciutto, and suggested that we stop and grab a Prosecco and some ham from him. But whose Prosecco?

Then the wine list was laid on the table. At last, I thought, I will be schooled. Valentino accepted the list and, without opening it, handed it to me. "Oh, is that the plan?" I muttered to myself. "Let the new guy choose the wines, then pick apart his choices." We had been served a *salumi* plate, and *casoncelli,* the local meat-filled ravioli, were arriving next. There would also be some braised meat. I nervously chose two bottles: one white, Gravner Breg, and one red, Paolo Scavino Barolo Carobric. At least I will get to taste some good wine, I thought, before my choices are ripped to shreds by the experts.

The wine came. I tasted. They all tasted, and there were nods of agreement. The conversation resumed. From what I could gather, some loved the wine, others maybe not so much, but everyone enjoyed the evening. There was no critique. I was puzzled that these two men, arguably among the top wine experts in Lombardy, didn't say a word about the wine.

On the car ride back to the hotel, I asked Marc if Valentino and Alberto had said anything about the wine I didn't understand. "Nothing at all," he said. "For most of the night, we were all just catching up." The food was fantastic and the wine was incredible, but they were bit parts in the evening's production. The star of the night was a group of ten old friends reunited and taking pleasure in one another's company. Valentino invited me to pick the wine because he knew I would enjoy doing so—nothing more, nothing less. With that gesture, Valentino taught me an important lesson: The ideal choice is more than its technical aspects. It is also the one that best serves the occasion.

Valentino

The next day we drove to Verona, where Vinitaly, attended by the country's most prominent winemakers, was being held in a series of ten airplane hangars. With all of these fabulous wines before us, I was certain that Alberto would suggest wines to try. Instead, he introduced us to his friends and talked more about the vineyards and winemakers than he talked about the wine. Although I didn't know it at the time, this was another step in my wine education. I met many welcoming winemakers that day, including Francesca Planeta, the Sicilian winemaker Alberto had mentioned the previous evening. After a wonderful conversation and a glass of her Chardonnay, I even decided to carry Planeta wines at Vetri.

Two days later, Marc and I flew back home to Philadelphia. By Christmas 1999, Planeta was named winery of the year by Gambero Rosso, the pinnacle of Italian wine ratings. We were proud to be carrying Planeta wines, and I was thrilled to have met and talked with Francesca herself! This was lesson number two. All ten hangars at Vinitaly had been filled with good wine, many of them outstanding, some of them less so. But I had managed to make a personal connection with the makers of some of the finest offerings.

Finally, I understood what Valentino Rossi and Alberto Galeati do. They forge meaningful relationships with wine. They visit vineyards all over Italy and Europe and talk to winemakers, absorbing as much as possible about the wines and the people

who make them. They helped me understand that I must do the same thing as wine director at Vetri and Osteria. Every bottle of wine has a story, and it is my responsibility to know the story and to let our customers know it.

BEYOND WINE LABELS

I know that not everyone can have a personal connection to the wines they choose. But it can be developed. If you feel unfamiliar with wine, just jump in and drink more of it. Read about it and talk about it. Visit vineyards and chat with the winemakers. In no time, you will find yourself using the language of wine. You will feel the weight of a wine in your mouth and call it light, medium, or heavy. You will identify spice flavors like licorice and black pepper, herbal aromas like grass and mown hay, fruit flavors like banana and plum, and earth flavors like flint and steel. You will sense the lingering aromas of aging, like vanilla, tar, and truffles.

Keep an open mind. Avoid writing off entire regions or grapes, such as Chardonnays, because they are not trendy. Indeed, some Chardonnays are outstanding. Explore and have fun. Wine pairing is not an academic exercise. It should be enjoyable.

Whenever you are faced with a wine choice, ask yourself a few simple questions. What kind of meal am I having? Is it an anniversary celebration or a business dinner? Is it at home or at a fancy restaurant? Do I want to taste something spectacular, or do I want an easy-drinking beverage? Do I want to stick with an old favorite or try something new? What flavors do I want to taste? What is my budget? But the most important question is, which wine would make this particular moment as enjoyable and memorable as possible? That is the wine to choose.

I asked myself these kinds of questions when deciding on wine pairings for the recipes in this book. I found myself suggesting many wines with which I have a personal relationship, and I sometimes explain that link along with the objective qualities of the choice, so you understand the selection. I have often included more than one option for each dish, which allows you to make a personal choice, and I have reached into cellars beyond Italy.

Above all, I urge you to look beyond wine labels and the technical aspects of the beverage. Whenever I find myself getting too analytical about wine pairings, I think back to my most memorable meal with Valentino Rossi and Alberto Galeati. It was in 2003 at Osteria della Brughiera, a Bergamo restaurant, and the old crew was reunited, including Marc, Marco Rossi, Luca and Cinzia Brasi, Massi Locatelli, and Valentino Rossi. Alberto Galeati and his wife, Laura, brought their new baby boy, Julio, to the dinner, and the entire table was excited to see the *bambino*. I fretted over the wine choice, calculating the various options for this special meal. Finally, on a whim, I ordered a bottle of Radikon Ribolla Gialla. Everyone was eating, laughing, drinking, reminiscing, and marveling at the baby. The wine tasted fabulous with the food. But at that moment, the most important beverage on the table was the little boy's bottle of milk. That evening was Julio's moment to shine, and the wine merely served to enhance the moment.

Following pages: Marc and Valentino
at the Monzio Compagnoni winery

I. THE FAMILY

la famiglia

Every once in a while, if you're lucky, you meet people who change your life forever. When I first went to Italy to cook, I was fortunate to meet a handful of people who were eventually woven into my very heart and soul. These are the people who mentored, inspired, and motivated me when I worked in Bergamo, in Lombardy. They taught me to approach food with simplicity and respect, and they continue to shape my thinking every time I return to Italy. At one time or another, we all worked at Taverna Colleoni dell'Angelo, a magnificent yet unpretentious restaurant on the Piazza Vecchia in Bergamo's high city. Those who no longer work there have since opened their own successful restaurants and shops. These people are the lifeblood of Bergamo, and they personify the style of cooking that I embrace.

Pierangelo Cornaro

THE BOSS *il boss*

Pierangelo is one of the most accomplished chefs I know. He grew up in a restaurant family in Bergamo, cooked all over Europe, and returned to Bergamo to open Antico Ristorante dell'Angelo, which soon earned two stars from Michelin. In 1976, Pierangelo took over for his father at Taverna Colleoni dell'Angello. There, he established a new kind of cuisine that skillfully blended regional traditions with current restaurant trends. In 1980, he was the only Italian chef invited to La Jeune Gastronomie, a world-renowned culinary competition hosted by New York's American Institute of Wine and Food. Pierangelo's unexpected success was hailed in the *New York Times*, the *Washington Post*, the *Chicago Tribune*, and elsewhere, expanding the taverna's already enviable reputation. He has since taught courses on Italian cuisine everywhere from the Italian Culinary Institute in Turin to the Robert Mondavi Winery in Napa, California.

With his son, Nevio, Pierangelo continues to expand his Italian culinary heritage. Everyone in Bergamo calls him the Boss, and his Taverna Colleoni dell'Angelo has become a prominent training ground for chefs. Cooks from around the world travel there to work, and in turn, the Boss sends his chefs around the world. Many have gone on to open award-winning restaurants of their own.

The Boss is a magnanimous soul. When I was working at the taverna, after dinner service, he regularly stayed up until three or four in the morning telling story after story about restaurants he had trained in, chefs he had learned from, and cooks he had taught. He would show us cookbooks, give us lessons, and make us laugh. Everyone respects him. The most valuable thing he taught me was to be serious about food.

Graziano Pinato

THE CHEF *il cuoco*

Born and raised in Bergamo, Graziano Pinato is the chef of chefs. He has been cooking at Taverna Colleoni dell'Angelo for more than twenty-five years, and now that the Boss works the front of the house, Graziano is the head chef. He is the single most important influence on my cooking and the most proud, genuine man I have ever met.

Graziano shares everything and hides nothing. There were never any secrets in his kitchen. He wants nothing more than to get other people excited about the subtleties of his craft. Whenever a special ingredient came in—from kid to fresh turbot to truffles—Graziano would take me aside to explain it to me. After preparing the day's dishes for the menu, he would make extra dishes to show me the numerous ways of seeing and preparing the same food. He took me to farms. He scheduled visits to butchers. He sent me to restaurants. Graziano put my hands deep into the world of fine food. Whenever we had a day off, he would pack me a take-home lunch because he knew I had no money. He was like a father and a brother to me.

I cooked with Graziano for a year and he taught me what it means to be a chef. Or, more important, what being a chef doesn't mean. It doesn't mean being a technical wizard. It doesn't mean obsessing over stars and great reviews. It means you cook with your heart. For example, Graziano explained that when you prepare meat, you should think about the animal, the environment in which it was raised, and what it ate, so that you pay tribute to the animal's life and make your dish the best it can be. The same is true for fish, poultry, vegetables, and every food that comes from the earth. Graziano taught me that being a chef means understanding all facets of food, respecting the ingredients you are working with, and honoring them to the best of your culinary ability.

Marco Rossi

THE PASSIONATE ONE

Marco has more passion in his pinky finger than most people have in their whole body. In 1994, we worked together at Taverna Colleoni and became good friends. He was a waiter, and you could immediately tell how much the Boss liked him. People even thought he was his son. With Marco, the Boss laughed his deepest and shared his most private side. Marco has a charisma that people cannot resist.

Marco is a successful restaurateur as well. He studied at the prestigious San Pellegrino hotel school, put in some time at a Marriott hotel in Boston, and worked for Pierangelo at Antico Ristorante dell'Angelo. My friend Luca Brasi calls him a phenomenon. Whatever he touches turns to gold. In 1999, the same year I opened Vetri, Marco took over Le Cantine D, a restaurant above a wine store in Bergamo. It became an instant success. A few years later, Marco moved the restaurant downstairs to be closer to the wine store and renamed it L'Osteria. Another instant success.

Marco was born and raised in Bergamo, and every time I return there, we stay up late talking for hours about food, music, movies, and just about everything. His lust for life inspires me to trust myself and follow my own vision. A lot of my passion for cooking comes from working with Marco.

l'appassionato

Massimiliana Locatelli

THE ARTIST *l'artista*

Massi was the soul of Taverna Colleoni. Originally from France, she moved to Bergamo when she was in her twenties. When we worked together in 1994, Massi was the oil that made the restaurant's engine run. She organized all of the restaurant's parties, kept all of the books, handled the flowers, answered the phone, and designed the menus. She is the most creative restaurant manager I have ever known. Eventually, her talents grew too big for the job she was doing, and Massi went to work for a graphic design company. In 1998, she opened her own shop, Artementi, on Via Mario Lupo in Bergamo's high city. To this day, she designs incredible menus, cards, signs, and more.

Massi is such a close friend that I feel I am an extension of her creativity. Whenever I come up with something new for Vetri or Osteria, the idea seems willed to me through her. She creates all of the menus, business cards, and other designs for Vetri and Osteria.

Paolo Frosio

THE TALENT *il virtuoso*

In 1990, at the age of twenty-three, Paolo Frosio opened Frosio Ristorante in the small town of Alme, just outside of Bergamo. In his second year, he earned a Michelin star and became Italy's youngest ever Michelin-star chef.

Born into a family of restaurateurs in Valle Imagna, in Bergamo Province, Paolo honed his skills at the San Pellegrino hotel school, intending to study agriculture later. But once he got in the kitchen, Paolo knew where he belonged. He trained with many notable chefs around the world, including Piero Selvaggio at Valentino in Los Angeles, and now runs Frosio Ristorante with his brother, Camillo. The Frosio family also owns a restaurant in the mountains outside Bergamo.

No chef I have worked with has inspired me more than Paolo Frosio. Every time I eat at his restaurant or work in his kitchen, I learn a new technique or discover a distinctive flavor combination. Paolo has an incredible palate and is singularly focused on surprising and delighting guests. Like the architecture of his restaurant, which was built in the 1700s and remodeled through the centuries, Paolo's food blends elements of both classic and contemporary cuisine. I'm always impressed by his ability to zero in on two ingredients and marry them in a single dish in a completely unique way.

Most of all, Paolo understands balance. Take, for example, his relationship with his brother and partner, Camillo. Paolo is the thinker. Camillo is the reactor. Paolo stays in the kitchen. Camillo stays in the dining room. Paolo knows that this kind of balance gives a restaurant its soul. He lives and breathes the life of a creative chef, always pushing himself to discover new dishes, new flavors, and new presentations.

Luca Brasi

THE VISIONARY *il visionario*

Another genius at the stove, Luca Brasi also has a keen eye for business. His father is a prominent businessman, and it was expected that Luca would follow in his father's footsteps. But Luca was stubborn. He wanted to go his own way and had a passion for cooking. His father sent him to work in a restaurant so Luca would understand how tiring and demanding it was to work all day in a kitchen. The plan backfired. Working the line, Luca's passion blossomed and he found his true path in life.

Luca developed his culinary skill at the hotel school in Bergamo and refined his talent at Taverna Colleoni a few years before I arrived. Then he cooked throughout Switzerland, France, and Italy, eventually returning to Bergamo, where he restored an old trattoria in the historical center of Osio Sotto, updating the place with a clean, contemporary design. In 1997, he opened it as La Lucanda, a trendsetting restaurant and charming eight-room hotel. In the kitchen, Luca is swift, effortless, and brilliant. Like many successful Italian chefs, his food perfectly unites tradition with innovation. One of his signature dishes, *tortelli* with bitter almonds and black truffle, shows that food can be bold and unfussy at the same time.

In 2003, La Lucanda earned a Michelin star, and a year later, Luca opened Olfa café and *pasticceria* just down the street. In 2007, he sold the hotel-restaurant in Osio Sotto, including the name, and, with his wife, Cinzia, and son, Mateo, moved closer to Milan to run the one-hundred-room Hotel Devero and its three restaurants: the upscale La Lucanda, a more casual bistro-style restaurant, and another Olfa café and *pasticceria*.

Luca has taken some big risks in life, but they have all paid off. He is a humble man, soft-spoken and polite, but you can see the wheels turning, the ideas emerging, and the plans developing. During the many meals and conversations we have shared, Luca has proven to me that a passionate, creative person can also be a businessman.

2. THE JOURNEY

il viaggio

For as long as I can remember, I wanted to go to Italy. My paternal grandfather, Mario Vetri, was born in Sicily in the town of Enna in 1896. He left there in the 1920s, when the country was in the throes of a depression, immigrating to Philadelphia, where he happened to meet Jenny, the daughter of his neighbors in Enna. They married and my father, Sal, was born in 1936. I was born a generation later, in 1966. On Sundays, we would all go over to my grandparents' house just as the family had done in Sicily. There, we would cook, eat, share stories, and laugh. My grandmother Jenny made all sorts of Italian specialties, like meatballs, eggs in tomato sauce, ricotta cheesecake, and, of course, the seven-fish dinners at holiday time, with fried *baccalà* (salt cod), fried smelts, and fried squid. She also included a little meat like *braciole*.

That was my life growing up in Abington, Pennsylvania, just north of Center City Philadelphia. I played basketball, cooked with my family, played guitar. In 1990, I graduated from Drexel University with a degree in marketing and finance, but music was my passion, so I went to Los Angeles to study jazz guitar at the Musician's Institute of America. At school, I didn't have a lot of money, and I took a job cooking at the North Beach Bar and Grill to make ends meet. Cooking came naturally. I had always cooked with my parents and grandparents.

Miles Angelo was the chef at North Beach, and we worked together for a year. When I graduated from school, I had hoped Miles would give me a raise and a more permanent position, but he couldn't, so I decided it was time to move on. My band was trying to make a living playing music, but the gigs paid poorly. I heard Wolfgang Puck was opening a restaurant called Granita, and I inexplicably had a

strong urge to work there. What if I just knocked on the door? Would I be offered a job? I gave it a shot. I went to Granita every day for three weeks. Each time I asked the chef, Joseph Manzare, for a job. Each time, he would reply, "I don't have anything." But he was also encouraging, always adding, "Come back another day." The third week, one of his chefs called in sick at the last minute. Joseph yelled out the back door to me, "Do you want to hang around tonight?" I quickly accepted. That night, I worked the line, and after the shift, Joseph asked me if I wanted to come back the next day. I returned to the Granita kitchen every day for six weeks.

I had left North Beach and had very little money, and Joseph wasn't able to pay me anything. But I did eat at the restaurant, and I had saved enough money

to keep up with the rent. And every day, I went in, hoping Joseph would offer me a permanent job. Six weeks later, one of the cooks left, and Joseph immediately offered me the position. That year, Joseph Manzare became my mentor. He taught me all the basics I would have learned in culinary school: how to fillet a fish, simmer a rich stock, make reduction sauces, braise tough meats, poach delicate seafood, roast a chicken. Joseph opened my eyes to the beauty of food and guided my hands through the world of fine cuisine.

Joseph Manzare

For the next two years, I steeped myself in Granita and a few other California restaurants. I cooked at night and played guitar in the studio all day with my band. We were trying to record an album, but we weren't getting anywhere. I had also become restless with California cuisine. I was working as the morning chef at a place called Bambu when it dawned on me that the food I was cooking was soulless.

Every dish had an identity complex. Broccoli-hazelnut puree served under grilled salmon with a port wine reduction. Enoki mushrooms, black-eyed peas, and corn salsa. Do these things go together? Salsas were made out of everything. The pasta, fashioned from premade sheets, some thick, some thin, was awful. And almost every main course followed the same prescription: make a salsa, put a piece of fish on top, and then make a reduction sauce, whisk butter into it, and add it to the plate. Diners were applauding the food, but I thought it was terrible. I knew I had to get out of LA.

It was 1993, and Joseph had moved on to become the chef at Wolfgang Puck's Spago. We had become good friends and took a Tuesday-night class together in restaurant operations management. I had mentioned to him that I wanted to work in Italy, and one night after class, we stopped by Valentino restaurant, where he introduced me to the owner, Piero Selvaggio.

I told Piero that I had been cooking in California for a few years and was learning all about California cuisine, but that I really wanted to cook Italian. I told him about my Sicilian-born grandfather, Mario, about cooking on Sundays with my whole family, and about how I felt the need to cook in Italy. Piero didn't know me, but he trusted Joseph, and I guess he saw something in me. He told me he knew of a restaurant in northern Italy, in Bergamo, where I could work in the kitchen and live in an apartment the restaurant maintained for the cooks, and he would make some calls. A week went by and I hadn't heard anything, so I called Piero to ask him if he had talked to anyone. I think he was a little annoyed, but he wrote a note and told me to give it to the owner of a restaurant called Frosio, outside Bergamo. The note explained simply that I was a cook in LA and I wanted to work in Italy, and to "please help out any way you can," followed by Piero's signature. That note was all I had. No phone number. No place to stay. No guarantee that I would find work. But I knew I had to go to Italy, so I bought a one-way ticket to Bergamo and boarded a plane with the note and fifteen hundred dollars in my pocket.

After an eight-hour plane trip, a two-hour train ride, a night in a hotel, a one-hour bus journey, and a long walk with a lovely elderly woman who felt bad for me, I made it to Frosio Ristorante just in time for lunch. The chef, Paolo Frosio, spoke only a little English, and I knew very few Italian words. At first, Paolo didn't understand why I was there. I was wearing denim overalls and had a backpack flung over one shoulder and a guitar case slung over the other. Paolo looked down at the note, read through it, suddenly understood, and rolled his eyes. "What I am going to do with you?" he asked me. He looked at his brother, Camillo, and started yelling at him like it was his fault. Paolo knew Piero Selvaggio, so he felt he should help me, but he no longer had an apartment and couldn't give me work. Paolo pursed his lips, looked up, and said, "Go to Taverna. Talk to Pierangelo Cornaro."

Cooking al fresco in Bergamo, 1994

Camillo put me in a car and drove about thirty minutes to Taverna Colleoni dell'Angelo in Bergamo. The restaurant was in the high city, known as Bergamo Alta, a walled medieval hilltop town with steep cobblestone streets, majestic cathedrals, libraries, museums, shops, pubs, and piazzas. The restaurant's tan awning stretched across the northwest side of Piazza Vecchia, just a few steps away from the magnificent church of Santa Maria Maggiore, which has been turning out famous musicians since 1137.

Marc and Graziano

As we passed the eighteenth-century Contarini Fountain in the center of the piazza, a feeling in my heart grew stronger. We approached the restaurant, walked between the crisply set tables outside under the awning, and entered the main dining area, a regal room with vaulted ceilings, thick stone columns, and huge paintings on the walls. To the left, a black grand piano looked over a set of descending white marble stairs. The floor stretched in every direction with hexagonal terrazzo tiles of ivory, gold, and slate.

Leaning calmly against one of the stone columns was a man who looked like a cross between Napoleon Bonaparte and Tony Orlando. This was the Boss, Pierangelo Cornaro. Camillo said a few words to him, then I approached the man and handed him the note. He read it and started chuckling. A little smile emerged from his thick, cropped mustache and I knew this had happened to him before. He gazed up into the vaulted ceiling as he handed the note to his head chef, Graziano Pinato. They both started laughing. Graziano turned and looked me in the eye as if to tell me something, but he said nothing. Then, the Boss looked at one of his Canadian cooks in training and told him to take me to the restaurant's apartment and show me a bed.

That night, I returned to the taverna and started cooking. My journey in Italy had finally begun.

3. COLD APPETIZERS
antipasti freddi

My apartment in Bergamo was directly above Pub dell'Angelo, a local bar in the high city with beers on tap like Affligem, Wieckse Witte, and Murphy's. The dank front room was filled with spiky-haired punks and leather-clad women—a self-consciously edgy though not rough-and-tumble bar. I liked the idea of living above the place.

I had survived my first night of training at the Taverna Colleoni dell'Angelo and was eager for more. I walked up the winding cobblestone streets and across Piazza Vecchia to the taverna. When I strolled into the kitchen, the plating table stopped me in my tracks. It had been strewn with dishes for the servers the night before, so I hadn't noticed how large it was. My gaze moved down and the off-white floor tiles came into view. Each one was about two-feet square, with concentric maroon circles traversing it. I lifted my eyes and saw the huge vented hood running the length of the line, with burners and ovens below it and prep areas to the side. Now that the kitchen wasn't knee-deep in the dinner rush, it was easy to see everything. And I couldn't wait to get a knife back into my hands.

The Boss was leaning against a nearby doorway. He stood only five feet tall but had a commanding presence in his black suit, crisp white shirt, and red silk tie. He was always calm, always in control, his red-frame glasses, thick as Coke bottles, ensuring him a clear view of his world. He introduced me to the pasta chef, Stefano Terzi. Stefano made everything on the dinner menu that included flour: bread, pasta, puff pastry—you name it. One of the first dishes he showed me was an onion *crespella*, or crêpe. I sliced pound after pound of onions, and then cooked

them down over very low heat until they were deeply caramelized and their sweet, toasted aroma perfumed the entire kitchen. Stefano told me the crêpe-batter proportions and I made dozens of crêpes, ready to be filled when orders came in during dinner.

I watched some of the other cooks prepare their dishes. One of them was compressing eggplant strips under a sheet pan to rid them of excess moisture. Then he sautéed the strips until they were the color of caramel. He filled a mold with the cooked eggplant, drizzling every layer with a mixture of cream, eggs, Parmesan, and thyme, and baked the mold in a bain-marie. When it was done, he weighted it and chilled the whole thing. As the antipasto orders began coming in, he unmolded and sliced the eggplant terrine.

I couldn't believe how beautiful—and how simple—it was. I had only ever used eggplant to make ratatouille for serving as a side dish. I had never thought of using it in its own composed dish.

That day, I watched the other cooks prepare their dishes, too, and I learned many things. But the eggplant terrine taught me the best lesson: creativity is what keeps a restaurant alive. If you can take two eggplants and transform them into something spectacular, you have done something impressive.

EGGPLANT TERRINE 37
terrina di melanzane

ARTICHOKE SALAD 39
insalata di carciofi

SPRING PEAS WITH WALNUTS AND FRESH SHEEP'S MILK RICOTTA 40
piselli con noci e ricotta fresca di pecora

TOMATO FLAN WITH CRAB AND BASIL 41
sformato freddo di pomodori con granchio e basilico

PICKLED SARDINES 42
sardine marinate

OYSTERS WITH LEMON GELATO 45
ostriche con gelato al limone

NANTUCKET BAY SCALLOP CARPACCIO WITH LEMON AND FRIED PARSNIPS 47
carpaccio di capesante del Nantucket con limone e pastinache

SEAFOOD POACHED IN OLIVE OIL WITH RADICCHIO AND ASPARAGUS MAYONNAISE 48
crostacei cotti in olio con radicchio e maionese di asparagi

MARINATED SWORDFISH BRESAOLA WITH BASIL BREAD CRUMBS AND BALSAMIC 51
bresaola di pesce spada con pane grattuggiato al basilico e aceto balsamico

FOIE GRAS PASTRAMI WITH PEAR MOSTARDA AND BRIOCHE 53
pastrami di fegato d'anatra con mostarda di pere e brioscia

RUSTIC CHICKEN LIVER PÂTÉ ON CROSTINI 55
crostini di fegatini di pollo

WILD BOAR SALAMI 56
salame cotto di cinghiale

HOMEMADE BRESAOLA WITH MELON AND ARUGULA 59
bresaola nostrana con melone e rucola

SLOW-ROASTED PORK SLICES WITH TUNA SAUCE 60
porchetta tonnato

VENISON TARTARE WITH EGG YOLK 62
tartare di cervo con tuorlo d'uovo

EGGPLANT TERRINE

If you don't like eggplant, this preparation may change your mind. Salting, compressing, and sautéing the eggplant is time-consuming, but the results are remarkable. When you layer the compressed eggplant slices in a mold with cream, egg, and Parmesan, you end up with a rich, custardlike texture. Serve with sliced or chopped heirloom tomatoes and slivers of Parmesan. (Photo on page 33.) **Makes 10 to 12 servings**

> 2 large eggplants (about 5 pounds total)
> 4 cups water
> 1/2 cup kosher salt
> 1 teaspoon white wine vinegar
> 1 cup grape seed oil
> 1 large egg
> 1/4 cup heavy cream
> 2 tablespoons grated Parmesan cheese
> 1 1/2 tablespoons fresh thyme leaves
> Kosher salt and freshly ground black pepper
> 1 large heirloom tomato, coarsely chopped
> 1 ounce (1 cup) microgreens or baby arugula leaves
> 1 tablespoon extra virgin olive oil
> 10 to 12 very thin slices (shavings) Parmesan cheese

Using a vegetable peeler, remove the skin from the eggplant in long strips at least 1 inch wide. In a saucepan, combine the water, 2 tablespoons of the salt, and the vinegar and bring to a boil over medium-high heat. Add the eggplant-skin strips and boil for 5 minutes. Transfer to ice water to stop the cooking, and then drain and reserve.

Slice the eggplants into rounds about 1/8 inch thick. Sprinkle the rounds on both sides with the remaining 6 tablespoons salt. Place them on a rack over a sheet pan or in the sink and let stand for 1 hour.

Rinse the eggplant slices thoroughly under cold running water, and put them on a sheet pan lined with paper towels. Top the slices with more paper towels and a second sheet pan, and then weight the top pan with large cans of tomatoes or other heavy weights. Let stand for 1 hour.

Heat 2 tablespoons of the oil in a large sauté pan over medium-high heat. Add the eggplant slices in batches, using more oil as needed, and cook, turning once, for 2 to 3 minutes on each side, or until lightly browned on both sides. Drain on paper towels.

Preheat the oven to 375°F. In a bowl, whisk together the egg, cream, Parmesan, and thyme. Season lightly with salt and pepper. Line a 4- to 6-cup terrine or other mold with plastic wrap, allowing enough overhang on the sides to cover the filled mold. Then line the mold with the reserved eggplant skins to cover the bottom and sides completely (you may not need all of them). Layer the cooked eggplant slices in the lined mold, covering each layer with a drizzle of the egg mixture. Once the mold is full, fold the plastic wrap over the top.

Place the terrine in a roasting pan, and pour hot water into the pan to come about halfway up the sides of the mold. Cover the roasting pan with aluminum foil and bake for 1 hour, until the terrine springs back when pressed lightly.

Remove the pan from the oven, and remove the mold from the water bath. Place 1 or more heavy weights on the terrine and let cool to room temperature. Cover with plastic wrap and refrigerate with the weight(s) in place until cold, about 1 hour.

To serve, remove the weight(s), pull back the plastic wrap, and invert the terrine onto a cutting board. Lift off the mold and peel away the plastic wrap. Cut into 1/4-inch-thick slices and serve cold. Garnish with the tomato, arugula, olive oil, and Parmesan shavings.

PREP AHEAD
The eggplant terrine can be fully prepared and refrigerated for up to 2 days. Unmold just before serving.

VINO ·

> Layers of flavor make this a versatile dish for wine pairing. If you serve tomatoes on the side as suggested in the headnote, their acid will need mellowing. For a red wine, I would look to the most food-friendly grape available, Barbera. Bruno Giacosa Barbera d'Alba, an older style that is well balanced and less extracted, would do nicely. For a white, I like the fresh, grassy character of San Lorenzo Vernaccia di San Gimignano. —J.B.

ARTICHOKE SALAD

People always ask me how I prepare the artichokes for this salad. When I tell them the artichokes are raw, they get a funny look on their faces that suggests they don't believe me. That's because they are used to cooking large artichokes that need their pointy leaf spikes snipped off and their fuzzy chokes scraped away. But with baby artichokes, none of that is necessary. Just trim off the outer green leaves and thinly slice the interior yellow ones, and you can serve the artichokes as a salad. These babies are hard to find (farmers' markets are your best bet), but they make all the difference here. This dish is a perfect example of an elegant simplicity that defines my food. **Makes 4 servings**

Juice of 4 lemons (about 1/2 cup)
12 baby artichokes (about 11/2 pounds)
1/4 cup extra virgin olive oil
Kosher salt and freshly ground black pepper
1 ounce (1 cup) baby arugula leaves
12 to 16 very thin slices (shavings) Parmesan cheese

Squeeze the lemon juice into a bowl. Working with 1 artichoke at a time, snap off the tough outer green leaves until you are left with a small bullet-shaped artichoke with pale yellow leaves that turn green just at the tips. Cut off the green tips crosswise. Cut the stem flush with the bottom of the artichoke so that no green remains, cut the artichoke in half lengthwise, and scoop out and discard any choke. Then slice the artichoke halves lengthwise as thinly as possible and immediately toss the pieces into the lemon juice to inhibit browning.

When all of the artichokes are sliced, add the oil, season with salt and pepper, and mix thoroughly. Arrange the arugula leaves on individual plates and spoon the artichoke in the center. Garnish with the Parmesan.

PREP AHEAD
The artichoke mixture can be made up to 5 hours ahead of time, covered, and refrigerated. Arrange the salad on plates and garnish with the Parmesan just before serving.

VINO ·

Matching wine with artichokes is tough because they tend to sweeten everything. However, choosing a bone-dry wine that is almost too dry to drink on its own is a good solution. Because this dish is served at the beginning of the meal, you need a wine that is easy to drink and not too complex. Verdicchios from the Marche work well. They aren't overly fruity, and they show off great minerality that is just shy of briny on the palate. Sartarelli Verdicchio dei Castelli di Jesi consistently tops my list. —J.B.

SPRING PEAS WITH WALNUTS AND FRESH SHEEP'S MILK RICOTTA

Great cooking is all about great ingredients. In the right season, these flavorful vegetables and a top-drawer cheese are magical. The very same dish with so-so vegetables and an ordinary cheese can taste like the worst antipasto you have ever been served. The cheese here must be fresh and creamy. Ricotta purchased in a tub at the supermarket simply won't do. Look for an imported sheep's or cow's milk ricotta from one of the purveyors in the Sources section (page 280). Serve with warm bruschetta. **Makes 4 servings**

> **2 pounds English peas, removed from the pod**
> **1 tablespoon sherry vinegar**
> **1 tablespoon walnut oil**
> **1/2 cup extra virgin olive oil**
> **1/2 cup chopped black walnuts**
> **Kosher salt and freshly ground black pepper**
> **1/2 cup best-quality imported sheep's or cow's milk ricotta cheese**

Bring a large pot of salted water to a boil. Add the peas and blanch for 1 1/2 minutes. Transfer to ice water to stop the cooking. Once cool, use your fingers to slip the peas from their skins. You should have about 2 cups shelled peas.

In a bowl, whisk together the vinegar, walnut oil, and olive oil. Stir in the peas and walnuts, and season with salt and pepper.

Divide the ricotta evenly among chilled plates, placing a dollop in the center of each plate. Make a well in the center of each dollop of ricotta, and spoon some of the pea mixture into the wells. Spoon the remaining pea mixture around the ricotta.

IMPROV
Substitute 1 pound of fava beans, removed from the pod, for half of the peas. Blanch the beans for 1 1/2 minutes, transfer to ice water to stop cooking, and slip off their tough skins once they are cool.

VINO ·

A case can be made for serving a buttery Chardonnay here because a little creaminess complements the walnuts. However, the ricotta already provides a good deal of creaminess, mellowing the overall flavor profile. A Chardonnay is still my choice, but I would head to Burgundy for a nutty, dry, minerally Chablis, with Jean Dauvissat Montmains my preferred selection. —J.B.

TOMATO FLAN WITH CRAB AND BASIL

A few years ago, Vetri sous chef Brad Spence enjoyed a tomato flan while eating in and around Florence. When he got back to America, we experimented with various ways of serving the flan, and this was our favorite. Apart from oil and vinegar, the tomato, basil, and crab are the only flavors. Wait for the height of tomato season to make this refreshing dish. **Makes 6 servings**

CRAB AND BASIL

1 pound jumbo lump crabmeat, picked clean of any shells or cartilage

1/4 cup extra virgin olive oil

Juice of 1/2 lemon

3 tablespoons fresh baby basil leaves or finely shredded full-sized basil leaves

Kosher salt and freshly ground black pepper

TOMATO FLAN

3 ripe heirloom tomatoes (about 11/2 pounds total), cored and sliced

1/4 white onion, chopped

Kosher salt and freshly ground black pepper

1/4 cup extra virgin olive oil

1/4 teaspoon sherry vinegar

11/2 sheets gelatin or 11/2 teaspoons (1/8 ounce) powdered gelatin

For the crab and basil: Put the crab, oil, lemon juice, and 11/2 tablespoons of the basil in a small bowl. Season with salt and pepper and toss gently to combine. Cover and refrigerate for 4 to 6 hours. Reserve the remaining 1/2 tablespoon basil for garnish.

For the tomato flan: Put the tomatoes and onion in a bowl, season with salt and pepper, and toss gently. Let stand for 10 minutes, then transfer the mixture to a blender and process until emulsified well. With the machine running, drizzle in the oil and vinegar and process until smooth.

Put the gelatin sheets in a bowl of cold water and let stand for about 5 minutes, or until softened. Drain the sheets, squeeze out any excess moisture, and then place them in the top of a double boiler. (If using powdered gelatin, sprinkle the gelatin over 2 tablespoons cold water in the top of a double boiler and let stand for 3 to 5 minutes, or until softened.) Measure out 11/2 cups of the tomato mixture and add to the gelatin. Place over (not touching) simmering water in the lower pan and heat, stirring, until warm and well combined. Do not allow to boil. Strain the mixture through a fine-mesh sieve into a bowl.

Oil six 1/2-cup soufflé tins. Fill the tins almost full with the tomato mixture. Cover and refrigerate until set, about 1 day.

To finish: Run a knife around the edges of the flans, wrap the bottoms in a warm towel, then unmold the flans onto individual plates. Garnish the flans with the crab salad and the remaining 1/2 tablespoon basil.

PREP AHEAD

The flans can be made up to 1 day ahead, covered, and refrigerated. Unmold just before serving.

IMPROV

If you like, serve this dish as gazpacho instead of flan. Omit the onion and gelatin and season the tomatoes in a bowl as directed. Chop 1 of the tomatoes and set aside. Puree the remainder in a blender until smooth. Strain the puree through a fine-mesh sieve into a bowl, and add the chopped tomatoes and some finely diced cucumber, red bell pepper, sweet onion, and shallot. Ladle into bowls, spoon the crab on top, and garnish with the remaining basil.

VINO ·

Let's go straight to Venetian whites here. With the acidic tomato, I like Soave Classico best. Roberto Anselmi (who declassified his wines) makes a wine called Capitel Croce that works exceptionally well. For a lighter, crisper Garganega, try Allegrini Soave. It exhibits pronounced minerality and has an ultracrisp texture from its time spent in stainless steel. —J.B.

PICKLED SARDINES

When you have truly fresh sardines, a brief soak in some pickling liquid is the best way to showcase them. There is no cooking, so it is impossible to overcook the fish. But be careful not to overmarinate them, or the flesh will dry out from the salt. One hour is plenty. I like to use relatively small sardines, about 3 ounces each. If you buy larger ones, let them marinate a bit longer. **Makes 6 servings (about 1 quart)**

10 small sardines (3 to 4 ounces each)

1 1/2 cups water

1 cup white wine vinegar

1/4 cup sugar

1 tablespoon kosher salt

1 bay leaf

10 black peppercorns

1 teaspoon chili flakes

1 small red onion, julienned

4 cloves garlic, smashed

1 carrot, peeled and cut into slabs 1/2 inch wide, 2 inches long, and 1/8 inch thick

2 celery stalks, one cut into slabs 1/8 inch wide, 2 inches long, and 1/8 inch thick, plus celery leaves for garnish

3 tablespoons extra virgin olive oil

2 teaspoons chopped fresh parsley

To fillet the sardines, 1 at a time, make a slit along the belly and remove and discard the entrails. Then deepen the slit, cutting all the way to the backbone. Remove the head and tail by cutting crosswise. Open up the fish so it lies almost flat and feel for the backbone near the head end. Slip your finger underneath the backbone (the flesh will be soft), grab it, and ease it away from the length of the fish, exposing the 2 sides (fillets). The smaller bones will come off with the backbone, and the rest of the fish is edible. Separate the fillets, or leave them attached if you prefer.

Lay the sardine fillets skin side up in a glass baking dish. In a bowl, mix together the water, vinegar, sugar, salt, bay leaf, peppercorns, chili flakes, onion, garlic, carrot, and julienned celery, stirring to dissolve the sugar. Pour the mixture over the sardines. Cover and marinate in the refrigerator for 1 hour.

Pour off and discard the liquid. Drizzle the sardines and vegetables with the oil. Using a vegetable peeler, shave the remaining celery into strips and immerse in ice water for 5 to 10 minutes, or until curled. Divide the vegetables among plates and top each plate with three sardine fillets. Garnish with the curled celery, celery leaves, chopped parsley, and some of the olive oil from the baking dish.

PREP AHEAD

After you pour off the liquid, you can drizzle the sardines with oil and refrigerate them for up to 3 days before serving.

VINO ·

At Vetri, we carry a declassified *vinho verde* that I particularly like with this dish. It is from Quinto do Feital, in Portugal's Minho region, and it is called Auratus. Slightly lower in alcohol than other *vinho verdes*, its strong minerality matches the sardines perfectly, plus it has a peach-fuzz feel that works nicely with the pickling spices. If you prefer a fuller-bodied Sauvignon Blanc, I suggest a trip to California for a Duckhorn or a Stags' Leap. —J.B.

OYSTERS WITH LEMON GELATO

While working at Taverna Colleoni dell'Angelo in 1994, I became friends with Peter Zambri, another chef in training. Peter eventually went to Victoria, British Columbia, where he opened Zambri's restaurant the same year I opened Vetri in Philadelphia. A few years later, I visited Peter at his restaurant, and he started the meal out with this oyster and gelato appetizer that blew my mind. I was so inspired, I made my own version the moment I got home. Try it. It seems a little out there at first, but the combination is fantastic. **Makes 6 servings**

> **24 oysters, preferably British Columbia oysters such as Gigamoto or Effingham**
>
> **Rock salt or crushed ice for serving**
>
> **¼ cup Lemon Crème Fraîche Gelato (page 264), softened (see Prep Ahead)**
>
> **4 chives, cut into ½-inch lengths**

Shuck the oysters by boring the pointed tip of an oyster knife or can opener into the hinged end of the shells and popping open the shells. Keep the shells flat to retain the oyster juices, then run a dull knife beneath the oysters to sever them from the shells. Leave the oysters in the half shell. Place the oysters on a bed of rock salt on a platter.

Dollop about ½ teaspoon of the gelato over each oyster. Place a chive length on each dollop.

PREP AHEAD
The gelato can be made up to 1 week in advance and kept frozen.

VINO

I recommend a sparkling wine for two reasons. First, you need something dry and crisp with the oysters, such as a brut. Second, this is the first dish of a multicourse meal, and you are likely to be drinking an *aperitivo*, which is probably a sparkling wine. I'm going to the Veneto for a Prosecco, which is a bit lighter than a Lombardian Franciacorta, a wine that would also work, but no less dry. Fermentation in stainless steel also gives Prosecco a minerality I appreciate with oysters. At Vetri, we pour Loredan Gasparini Prosecco. If you prefer a still wine, try a Bordeaux Blanc blend with Sauvignon Blanc and Sémillon, such as Pierre Lurton's terrific Château Marjosse. —J.B.

NANTUCKET BAY SCALLOP CARPACCIO WITH LEMON AND FRIED PARSNIPS

I get my scallops exclusively from Ken Brasfield of the Nantucket Specialty Seafood Company (see Sources, page 280). Ken is the best in the business, sending reports on the scallops' availability all year long. That's important because when the fall harvest begins, the supply may be limited and we will need to adjust our menu. You could use other small, fresh scallops, but Nantucket scallops have a creamy texture and sweet flavor all their own—like little wrapped candies. Putting heat on them would be a disservice. Raw is the only way to serve them. **Makes 4 servings**

> 1 small parsnip (3 to 4 ounces)
> Vegetable oil for frying
> Kosher salt and freshly ground black pepper
> 8 ounces Nantucket bay scallops
> Coarse sea salt such as *fleur de sel*
> Freshly cracked black pepper
> 1 tablespoon extra virgin olive oil
> 1 teaspoon fresh lemon juice
> 2 ounces (2 cups) microgreens or baby lettuces

Peel the parsnip with a vegetable peeler. Then use the peeler to create about 12 thin strips of parsnip, each 4 inches long and 1/4 to 1/2 inch wide.

Pour oil to a depth of about 1 1/2 inches into a deep, heavy skillet and heat to 350°F (or use a deep fryer). Add the parsnip strips in batches and fry, stirring occasionally, for 1 to 2 minutes, or until golden brown. Transfer the strips to paper towels to drain. Season with salt and pepper.

Slice the scallops as thinly as possible. Divide the slices among chilled plates, arranging them in a circle. Sprinkle with the coarse salt and cracked pepper, and then drizzle with the oil and lemon juice. Garnish with the fried parsnips and microgreens.

VINO ....

I can think of no better match here than Kuenhof Grüner Veltliner from Alto Adige. It has a subtle citrus flavor to complement the lemon and scallop and focused acidity to cut through the fried parsnips. While this wine may be hard to find, persistence will pay off. If you can't find it, look for one of the original Austrian versions of Grüner Veltliner from the Wachau. —J.B.

SEAFOOD POACHED IN OLIVE OIL WITH RADICCHIO AND ASPARAGUS MAYONNAISE

The first time I ate lobster poached in olive oil, I nearly fell out of my chair. Lobster is ethereal enough on its own, but poached in olive oil it becomes utterly extravagant. Here, fresh thyme in the oil lends a subtle fragrance, flavoring both the lobster and the turbot fillet that is also cooked in the oil. A scattering of mussels, a few bitter greens for punch, and some creamy mayonnaise and this dish is complete. **Makes 4 servings**

SEAFOOD
2 cups extra virgin olive oil

1 clove garlic

1 pound mussels, scrubbed and debearded

2 cups dry white wine

1 large lobster (about 1 1/2 pounds)

1 bunch thyme

1 turbot fillet (about 3 ounces)

ASPARAGUS MAYONNAISE
12 ounces asparagus, tough ends removed

1 large egg yolk

1 clove garlic

1 teaspoon sherry vinegar

1 cup extra virgin olive oil

Kosher salt and freshly ground black pepper

1 head radicchio, sliced

24 whole parsley leaves, plus 1 1/2 teaspoons chopped parsley

2 tablespoons extra virgin olive oil

For the seafood: Heat 1 tablespoon of the oil and the garlic in a wide, shallow sauté pan over medium-high heat. Add the mussels and wine, cover, and cook for about 3 minutes, or until the mussels open. Using a slotted spoon, remove the mussels from the liquid, discarding any mussels that failed to open and reserving the liquid. Pull the mussels from their shells and place them in a small bowl. Strain the reserved liquid through a fine-mesh sieve into the bowl. Cover and refrigerate until cold, about 1 hour.

To prepare the live lobster for cooking as quickly and painlessly as possible, put it on a cutting board and uncurl the tail so the lobster is flat. Position the tip of a chef's knife just behind the head and press down firmly until the knife tip reaches the cutting board, then bring the blade down between the eyes to finish the cut. Twist off the claws from the lobster and cut the lobster body crosswise to remove the tail from the rest of the body.

Put the remaining oil and the thyme in a small saucepan and heat over low heat to about 170°F. Add the tail and claws from the lobster to the oil and poach for 8 to 10 minutes, or until the shells turn bright pink. Remove the lobster pieces from the oil and set aside to cool. Then add the turbot to the hot oil and poach for 2 to 3 minutes, or until barely translucent in the center. Remove from the oil and set aside to cool.

When the lobster is cool enough to handle, crack the claws and remove the meat. Cut the tail in half lengthwise, remove the intestinal track, and lift out the meat. Let the meat cool, then cover and refrigerate the lobster and the turbot until cold, about 1 hour.

For the asparagus mayonnaise: Bring a wide, deep sauté pan filled with salted water to a boil. Add the asparagus and blanch for 1 minute. Immediately transfer to ice water to stop the cooking. Drain the asparagus, cut off the tips, and save for garnish. Coarsely chop the asparagus stalks and transfer to a food processor along with the egg yolk, garlic, and sherry vinegar. Process until smooth. With the machine running, slowly add the oil in a thin, steady stream and process until the mixture emulsifies. Transfer to a bowl, season with salt and pepper, and set aside, or cover and refrigerate if it will sit for more than 20 minutes.

continued on page 50

To finish: Let the mussels, lobster, turbot, and mayonnaise stand at room temperature for 20 minutes to take off the chill. Cut the lobster and turbot into bite-sized pieces. Spread the mayonnaise on plates and arrange the mussels, lobster, turbot, radicchio, and parsley leaves over the mayonnaise and season lightly with salt and pepper. Spoon the reserved mussel broth over the top and garnish with the reserved asparagus tips (if desired) and chopped parsley. Drizzle with the olive oil.

PREP AHEAD

The mayonnaise can be prepared up to a week in advance and the seafood up to 3 days in advance. Cover and refrigerate both until ready to serve.

VINO

A few years ago, you would be hard-pressed to find a sommelier saying, "How about a Slovenian wine?" But that's exactly what I am saying here, thanks in part to Aleš Kristančič from Brda, just over the border from Friuli. His wines, under the Movia label, are full bodied because they are harvested later and barrel-aged. He turns out an especially lush and fruity Tocai and Sauvignon Blanc, with my favorite the Veliko Belo, a blend of Chardonnay, Sauvignon Blanc, Pinot Grigio, and Ribolla Gialla that is big and fruity but keeps the oak in check. If you prefer a lighter wine, look for Kristančič's wines under the Villa Marija label, all of which are fermented in stainless steel. —J.B.

MARINATED SWORDFISH BRESAOLA
WITH BASIL BREAD CRUMBS AND BALSAMIC

This swordfish dish combines the process for making gravlax with the dry cure we use for our beef *bresaola* recipe. We use the same salt percentages and seasonings to achieve flavor, but we cure the fish for only 2 days, instead of the normal 10 days we use for beef. To make this dish, you will need a vacuum sealer (FoodSaver is a well-known brand), which can be found at big cookware stores or online (see Sources, page 280). **Makes 10 servings**

> 1 center-cut swordfish loin (3 pounds)
> 1 clove garlic, smashed
> 1/2 cup kosher salt
> 1/4 teaspoon ground cinnamon
> 1/4 teaspoon ground cloves
> 1/4 teaspoon freshly ground black pepper
> 1 cup plain dry bread crumbs
> 30 fresh basil leaves
> Best-quality balsamic vinegar
> Extra virgin olive oil

Pat the swordfish dry with paper towels. In a small bowl, stir together the garlic, salt, cinnamon, cloves, and pepper. Rub the mixture all over the swordfish, and then scatter any remaining mixture that doesn't adhere over a large piece of parchment paper. Wrap the parchment around the swordfish, place the packet on a rack set over a bowl (the fish will release a fair amount of liquid), and let rest at cool room temperature for 48 hours. Unwrap the fish, rinse with cool water, and pat dry. Vacuum package the fish and refrigerate for at least 2 days to finish the curing process.

Combine the bread crumbs and basil in a food processor and process until the bread crumbs look green. Sift the crumbs through a medium-mesh sieve into a small bowl.

Thinly slice the swordfish and lay 4 or 5 slices on each plate. Sprinkle with some basil bread crumbs and drizzle with the vinegar and oil.

PREP AHEAD
The vacuum-packaged fish will keep in the refrigerator for up to 2 weeks.

IMPROV
If you cannot find swordfish at the market, choose another large, firm-fleshed fish, such as tuna or shark.

VINO ·

> The salty component of this dish suggests a sparkling wine, but the fish, basil, and balsamic call for something creamier, with a fuller mouthfeel and less zest. Look for Château Beauchêne Côtes du Rhône Blanc, a great Rhône blend of Roussane and Marsanne grapes. Its honeysuckle palate nicely balances the balsamic vinegar, yet remains delicate enough for the fish. —J.B.

FOIE GRAS PASTRAMI WITH PEAR MOSTARDA AND BRIOCHE

Every year, I go out to Los Angeles to visit my brother, Adam. We rent motorcycles and usually ride up to Santa Barbara for tacos at La Super-Rica Taqueria. And then it is back to LA to shower and get ready for a twenty-five-course extravaganza at Spago. I have known Lee Hefter since before he started working for Wolfgang Puck, and I consider him one of the most talented chefs working today. On one of our Spago visits, he kicked off the meal with a foie gras pastrami— sweet, salty, rich, creamy—that floored me. Indeed, it was so good that Lee inspired me to make my own version for the Vetri menu. **Makes 12 to 15 servings**

> **3 quarts water**
> **1¹/₂ cups kosher salt**
> **¹/₂ cup sugar**
> **2 cloves garlic**
> **¹/₄ teaspoon ground cloves**
> **¹/₄ teaspoon garlic powder**
> **1 bay leaf**
> **18 ounces fresh foie gras**
> **1¹/₂ cups hickory wood chips**
> **¹/₄ cup coarsely ground coriander**
> **¹/₄ cup coarsely ground black pepper**
> **¹/₂ loaf Brioche (page 278)**
> **²/₃ cup (5 ounces) unsalted butter, softened**
> **³/₄ cup Pear Mostarda (page 275)**

In a saucepan, combine 1 quart of the water, the salt, and the sugar and heat over high heat, stirring, until the salt and sugar have dissolved. Remove from the heat and add the remaining 2 quarts water. Ladle out 1 cup of the mixture into a blender, add the garlic, cloves, garlic powder, and bay leaf, and process until the garlic and bay leaf are finely chopped. Pour the blended mixture back into the saucepan and let cool to room temperature.

continued on next page

Devein the foie gras by breaking 1 lobe at a time into small pieces and removing the veins. Roll or pack the deveined foie gras into roughly shaped balls bigger than a golf ball but smaller than a tennis ball (they will be slippery). Place the balls in the brine, cover, and refrigerate for 18 hours (or transfer the brine to a zippered plastic bag, add the balls, seal closed, and refrigerate).

Put the wood chips in a roasting pan, cover with cold water, and soak for 1 hour. Drain off the water completely.

Stir together the coriander and pepper in a bowl. Carefully remove the foie gras balls from the brine and pat dry. Roll the balls in the coriander mixture to coat evenly. Put the roasting pan of wood chips over high heat until you start to see smoke. Place a short roasting rack, cooling rack, or steamer basket over the chips and put the foie gras balls on the rack. Cover the pan (with foil if you have no lid), remove from the heat, and let stand for 10 minutes. Repeat this process of heating only the chips over high heat just until the smoke gets going, adding the rack of balls, and then removing from the heat 2 or 3 times, or just until the balls become soft to the touch and spreadable. Avoid overcooking the foie gras or it will melt and become grainy.

Line a 2-cup miniature loaf pan (about 5½ by 3 inches) with plastic wrap, allowing enough overhang on the sides to cover the filled pan. Place the cooked balls in the lined pan, and press down firmly with your hand or an offset spatula to squish the balls together. The foie gras should rise above the rim of the pan a little. Fold the plastic wrap over the top to cover, and then put a heavy weight, such a second loaf pan filled with rocks, on the foie gras to compact it in the pan. Refrigerate for 24 hours.

Cut the brioche into 12 to 15 slices about ¼ inch thick. Spread about 1 teaspoon of butter on each side. Toast the brioche on a griddle or large skillet over medium heat, turning once, for 2 to 3 minutes on each side, or until golden brown.

Cut each brioche slice on the diagonal into 2 triangles and put them on plates. Remove the weight from the loaf pan, fold back the plastic wrap, and invert the pan onto a cutting board. Lift off the pan and peel off the plastic wrap.

Cut the foie gras crosswise into slices about ¼ inch thick, and place the slices on the brioche triangles. Spoon the *mostarda* around the brioche.

PREP AHEAD

The foie gras will keep in the refrigerator up to 1 week.

VINO

Most sommeliers match foie gras with Sauternes because its sweet, sugary character plays well off the rich fat. Sometimes it can be a little cloying, however, and while the peppercorn and spice in the *mostarda* may call for a sweet wine, I prefer the Italian late harvests. The most accessible is *vin santo*, which can run from the mundane to the extraordinary. One of my favorites, a classic blend of Grechetto, Malvasia, and Trebbiano grapes, is from Avignonesi, the great producer of Vino Nobile. The sweetness is almost secondary, with flashes of vanilla and spice that accent the milkiness of the foie gras. For a bit less bling, try the Fattoria Felsina, a great vin santo with a touch of Sangiovese in it. —J.B.

RUSTIC CHICKEN LIVER PÂTÉ ON CROSTINI

Everywhere you travel in Italy, you will find different versions of chicken liver crostini. Some are chunky. Some are smooth. Some are served warm like a *ragù*. Mine is a rustic pâté made with butter, port, Cognac, rosemary, and sage and served chilled. I call it d'Angelo—"from the angel"—because I started making it when I was working at Taverna Colleoni dell'Angelo. Since then, the recipe has evolved, but it remains one of my favorite antipasti. **Makes 8 to 10 servings**

> 1¼ cups (10 ounces) plus 2 tablespoons unsalted butter, softened
>
> 1 small clove garlic
>
> 1¼ pounds chicken livers, trimmed of sinew and fat
>
> 1 rosemary sprig
>
> 1 sage sprig
>
> 2 ounces pancetta, finely chopped
>
> Kosher salt and freshly ground black pepper
>
> ¾ onion, julienned
>
> 2 tablespoons port
>
> 2 tablespoons Cognac
>
> 1½ teaspoons white truffle paste or ¼ to ½ teaspoon white truffle oil
>
> 18 slices country bread, toasted
>
> 2 tablespoons extra virgin olive oil

Melt 2 tablespoons of the butter in a sauté pan over medium heat. Add the garlic and cook for 2 minutes, or until golden. Add the chicken livers, rosemary, sage, and pancetta and cook, stirring, for 1 minute. Season with salt and pepper. Add the onion, reduce the heat to low, and sauté gently for 25 to 30 minutes, or until the livers are cooked and the onions are soft.

Pour in the port and Cognac, raise the heat to medium-high, and simmer until the liquid is reduced by about half. Remove from the heat and let cool to room temperature.

Remove and discard the herb stems from the liver mixture, and then transfer the mixture to a food processor. Add the remaining 1¼ cups butter and the truffle paste and process until a smooth puree forms. Taste and adjust the seasoning with salt and pepper. Pass the puree through a tamis or fine-mesh sieve into a bowl, and then cover and refrigerate until cold, about 1 hour.

Let the pâté stand at room temperature for 15 minutes to take off the chill. Top the toasted bread with the pâté and drizzle with the olive oil.

PREP AHEAD
The chicken liver pâté will keep in the refrigerator for up to 4 days.

VINO ·

Since this will be eaten as an antipasto or even an *amuse-bouche*, the right choice here is a Sercial Madeira, which can be drunk as an *aperitivo*. Sercial, which is inherently drier than Malmsey or Bual, is mellowed by the creamy sweetness of the liver. Charleston Sercial from The Rare Wine Co. is ideal. —J.B.

WILD BOAR SALAMI

Over the past few years, we have more than tripled the amount of *salumi* we make in-house. We installed a climate-controlled room in the basement that is filled with *soppressatta*, flat and rolled pancetta, *coppa*, *bresaola*, *culatello*, and other *salumi*. Many cured meats are complicated to make, but this recipe and the one for *bresaola* (page 59) can be made at home with relative ease. You will end up with 10 pounds of salami, which, depending on your salami consumption, may be perfect (it keeps refrigerated for about 2 weeks). If you prefer to make less, see Improv (below). You can purchase the beef bung (casing) and curing salt from sausage suppliers such as those listed in the Sources on page 280. This sausage calls for curing salt #1 (also known as T.C.M. or pink salt), a pink-colored salt that contains naturally occurring sodium nitrite to delay spoilage and maintain good color. Curing salt #1 is standard for cooked sausages. Other long-cured sausages often use curing salt #2, which contains sodium nitrate that's converted to sodium nitrite during the long cure. **Makes 10 pounds (40 to 50 servings)**

1 beef bung (about 18 inches long and 5 inches in diameter)

7 pounds boneless wild boar shoulder, cut into 1-inch pieces

3 pounds fatback, cut into 1-inch pieces

1/2 cup kosher salt

2 tablespoons sugar

1 1/2 tablespoons freshly ground black pepper

1 1/2 tablespoons ground coriander

2 teaspoons curing salt #1 (see headnote)

1 1/2 teaspoons chili flakes

4 cloves garlic, minced

1 cup ice water

2 quarts cold water

In a bowl, soak the beef bung in cold water to cover for at least 8 hours or up to overnight.

Put the meat and fatback in a bowl, cover, and freeze for about 1 hour, or until semifrozen. Using a meat grinder fitted with the largest die (3/8 to 1/2 inch), grind the meat and fatback, capturing them in a bowl. Add the kosher salt, sugar, pepper, coriander, curing salt, chili flakes, garlic, and ice water to the ground meat and fat. Using a stand mixer with the paddle attachment or a wooden spoon, mix thoroughly for about 2 minutes, or until thoroughly combined and somewhat sticky.

Drain the bung, and then stuff it with the meat mixture: hold one end, have someone hold the other end, and stuff in the meat as tightly as you can. Tie the ends with kitchen string. Then, using a straight pin, pop the air bubbles over the entire surface of the salami, working carefully to pierce them all.

In a deep pan, bring the cold water to a gentle simmer. Reduce the heat so the liquid shimmers just under a simmer (about 170°F). Submerge the salami in the liquid and cook until it reaches an internal temperature of 150°F. This will take 1 to 1 1/2 hours.

Transfer the salami to an ice bath and let cool completely. Drain, pat dry, and refrigerate until serving. Slice thinly to serve, making sure you remove the inedible casing.

PREP AHEAD
The salami will keep in the refrigerator for up to 2 weeks.

IMPROV
To make smaller salami and to make less (only about 2 1/2 pounds), replace the beef bung with beef middles and soak as directed. The middles, which are about 2 1/2 inches in diameter, can be cut to size, so you can make about 20 sausage links, each about 2 ounces. Most ingredients should be reduced to one-fourth the amount in the main recipe (you'll need a little less fatback and a little more pepper and coriander): 1 3/4 pounds boar shoulder, 8 ounces fatback, 2 tablespoons salt, 1 1/2 teaspoons sugar, 1 1/2 teaspoons freshly ground black pepper, 1 1/2 teaspoons ground coriander, 1/2 teaspoon curing salt #1, 1/2 teaspoon chili flakes, 1 clove garlic (minced), and 1/4 cup ice water. Proceed as directed, cooking the salami until they reach an internal temperature of 150°F. This will take about 1 hour.

VINO ·

Marc usually serves the boar salami with roasted figs and Parmesan shavings. If you serve it that way, you should look to a red wine accompaniment because the salami is cooked and somewhat gamey and a red wine will complement it and the figs. The relatively light, vibrant, dry fruit of Tomasso Bussola's entry level BG Valpolicella is superb this early in a meal. Or, the unfiltered style of Pecchenino Dolcetto di Dogliani would also work. The Dolcetto offers an earthiness and almost chocolate finish that marries with both the meat and the fruit. —J.B.

HOMEMADE BRESAOLA WITH MELON AND ARUGULA

Here's another cured meat recipe that is easy to make at home: rub the beef with a salt cure, chill it for 10 days, and then wrap it in cheesecloth and let it hang in your basement for 6 weeks. Simple. There is no better complement to slices of this chewy cured meat than chunks of juicy, sweet melon. I like to include some arugula for bite and some crusty bread. Look for the curing salt at a sausage supply house such as www.sausagemaker.com. **Makes about 5 pounds (20 to 25 servings)**

>   1 beef eye of the round (5 pounds)
>
>   3 tablespoons kosher salt
>
>   1 tablespoon sugar
>
>   1 teaspoon ground cumin
>
>   1 teaspoon freshly ground black pepper, plus extra for sprinkling
>
>   1 teaspoon chili flakes
>
>   1 teaspoon freshly grated nutmeg
>
>   1 teaspoon ground allspice
>
>   1 teaspoon curing salt #2 (see page 56)
>
>   1 ripe in-season melon such as Pancha, Crenshaw, or Canary, halved and seeded
>
>   1/2 bunch baby mint leaves
>
>   Extra virgin olive oil

Rinse the meat and pat dry thoroughly with paper towels. In a small bowl, stir together the kosher salt, sugar, cumin, pepper, chili flakes, nutmeg, allspice, and curing salt. Coat the meat thoroughly with the salt mixture. Place in a large zippered plastic bag, seal closed, and refrigerate for 10 days.

Remove the meat from the bag, rinse thoroughly, and pat dry. Wrap the meat in a double layer of cheesecloth and tie the open ends tightly with kitchen string. Hang the meat in a cool, dry place for 5 to 6 weeks, or until it feels firm to the touch. The ideal environment is 55° to 60°F and 70 to 75 percent humidity, as in a humid basement. As the meat ages, it will develop a rich aroma and a harmless white mold that can be scraped from the surface.

Thinly slice the *bresaola* and arrange on individual plates. Using a melon baller, scoop out melon balls from the melon halves and place on top. Garnish with the baby mint leaves and drizzle with the oil. Sprinkle with a little freshly ground black pepper on top.

PREP AHEAD

Once the *bresaola* has air-dried for about 6 weeks, it will keep in the refrigerator for about 1 week.

VINO ....

A *rosato* with some tartness works well here, such as Falesco Vitiano Rosato from Lazio. It is made with equal parts Sangiovese, Merlot, and Cabernet Sauvignon with a touch of Aleatico. The winery, owned by two of Italy's greatest oenologists, Renzo and Ricardo Cottarella, produces some of the finest and most underrated wines in the area. —J.B.

SLOW-ROASTED PORK SLICES WITH TUNA SAUCE

My version of the well-known Piedmont dish *vitello tonnato* (veal with tuna sauce) takes several departures. First, I use pork instead of veal, wrapping a pork belly around a pork loin. Second, the veal is traditionally braised, but I like to spit roast the pork instead to give it some crispy bits along with the tender, succulent meat. One thing I didn't mess with is the sauce. It's a classic tuna sauce with capers, lemon, egg yolk, and olive oil. This makes a great celebration dish for the holidays. **Makes about 20 servings**

PORK

6 quarts water

2 cups kosher salt

1 cup sugar

1 tablespoon curing salt #2 (see page 56)

2 cloves garlic

10 black peppercorns

5 rosemary sprigs

10 thyme sprigs

10 parsley stems

1 fresh bay leaf

1 boneless pork loin (1 1/2 pounds)

1 pork belly (about 9 pounds)

TUNA SAUCE

3 ounces best-quality imported olive oil–packed canned tuna (1/3 to 1/2 cup)

2 tablespoons drained capers

1 tablespoon white wine vinegar

1 tablespoon fresh lemon juice

1 large egg yolk

1 cup extra virgin olive oil

Kosher salt and freshly ground black pepper

15 arugula leaves

2 teaspoons fresh lemon juice

1 1/2 tablespoons extra virgin olive oil

Kosher salt and freshly ground black pepper

10 thin shavings Parmesan cheese

For the pork: Combine the water, kosher salt, sugar, and curing salt in a large roasting pan or a 2-gallon zippered plastic bag. Transfer 1 cup of the water to a blender and add the garlic, peppercorns, rosemary, thyme, parsley, and bay leaf. Process until the garlic and herbs are finely chopped. Pour the blended mixture back into the pan or bag.

Cut the pork loin lengthwise into halves or thirds to create smaller, narrower pieces that will fit end to end along the length of the belly. Add the pork belly and loin to the brine, cover or seal, and refrigerate for 3 days.

On the third day, remove the meat from the brine. Unfold the belly, lay it flat, and pat the belly and the loin pieces dry. Arrange the loin pieces end to end in a column along the length of the belly. Starting from a long end of the belly, tightly wrap the belly around the loin to make a long, narrow roll. Using kitchen string, tie the roll tightly at regular intervals in 9 or 10 places.

Prepare a medium fire (350°F) in a grill. (I use oak logs, but you can use charcoal or gas.) Secure the pork roll on a spit, tying it in a dozen or so places to make sure it is tight and rotates evenly. Spit roast the pork 8 to 12 inches above the fire for 1 1/2 to 2 hours, or until browned and crispy and the meat registers 145°F on an instant-read thermometer. Remove the pork from the spit and let cool.

For the tuna sauce: Put the tuna, capers, vinegar, lemon juice, and egg yolk in a blender and process until smooth. With the motor running, slowly add the oil in a thin, steady stream and process until the mixture is emulsified. The sauce should be somewhat thick yet pourable. If it is too thick, add a little water to thin it, and then season with salt and pepper.

To finish: Thinly slice the pork and lay a few slices on each plate. Spoon the tuna sauce over the pork. Toss the arugula with the lemon juice and oil and arrange over the pork. Season with salt and pepper and top with the Parmesan.

PREP AHEAD

After brining for 3 days, the meat can be removed from the brine and refrigerated for up to 2 days. After spit roasting, the meat can be refrigerated for about 1 month.

IMPROV

You can also cook the pork on a charcoal or gas grill over an indirect fire. You will need a grill rack with at least 24 inches in diameter of grill space (a 4- to 6-burner grill if using gas) to accommodate the pork. If your grill is smaller or if you want less meat, cut the recipe in half, using half of a pork belly and 12 ounces of pork loin.

To infuse the pork with a wood-smoke flavor, soak oak wood chips or chunks in water for 30 minutes and then toss a handful of the chips onto the hot coals of a charcoal grill, or put them in the smoker box of your gas grill and wait until you see smoke before you put the spitted pork over the fire or the pork directly on the grill rack. Apple wood is a nice change of pace from oak, giving the pork a flavor similar to apple wood–smoked bacon. You will have to replenish the chips or chunks once or twice during cooking.

VINO ···

This take on a Piedmontese classic calls for the rich white wines of the region—great wines too often outshined by their red counterparts. La Scolca Gavi di Gavi, which is traditionally produced from older vines, delivers a flinty palate and a nutty finish that balance out the creaminess of the sauce. —J.B.

VENISON TARTARE WITH EGG YOLK

Fresh, young venison tastes beautiful raw. I get mine from Broken Arrow Ranch in Texas. The deer live on an open range and eat a varied diet that gives the meat a complex flavor with minimal gaminess. The egg yolk adds richness, and the vinegar gives the dish a little spark. If you can find truffles, they will take this antipasto over the top. **Makes 4 servings**

> 8 ounces venison loin
>
> 1 tablespoon finely chopped mixed fresh herbs, such as rosemary, thyme, and flat-leaf parsley
>
> 3 tablespoons extra virgin olive oil
>
> 1 tablespoon sherry vinegar
>
> Kosher salt and freshly ground black pepper
>
> 2 ounces (2 cups) microgreens or baby lettuces
>
> 2 large egg yolks
>
> 1/2 ounce white truffle (optional)
>
> Parmesan cheese

Clean the venison of all sinew and fat (be vigilant; even a trace of sinew can ruin the texture). Then, using a butcher's knife, finely chop the meat. In a bowl, combine the meat, herbs, oil, and vinegar and mix until thoroughly combined. Season with salt and pepper.

Divide the meat mixture among chilled plates, and spread into a somewhat flat circle. Place the microgreens along the edge of the circle. In a bowl, whisk the egg yolks until very smooth and fluid, and then drizzle over the top of each serving. Using a vegetable peeler, shave an equal amount of the truffle over each serving. Then shave the cheese over the top. If serving as a tasting portion (as shown in the photo), divide the venison among deep-bowled spoons, drizzle on the egg yolks, shave the truffle and Parmesan over each spoon, and garnish with a smaller amount of microgreens.

VINO ·

You need some earth, dark fruit, and a bit of tobacco in the wine for both the venison and the truffle. Barbaresco works well, but I prefer a Syrah for its aromas of leather, smoke, and pepper. My preference is a Rhône Valley Hermitage from Jean-Louis Chave, but it isn't always available and it is pricey. For something lighter—and less costly—the Jean-Louis Chave Saint-Joseph Offerus is a good choice. It marries well with this dish, and its lighter body leaves open the red-wine possibilities for the rest of the meal. —J.B.

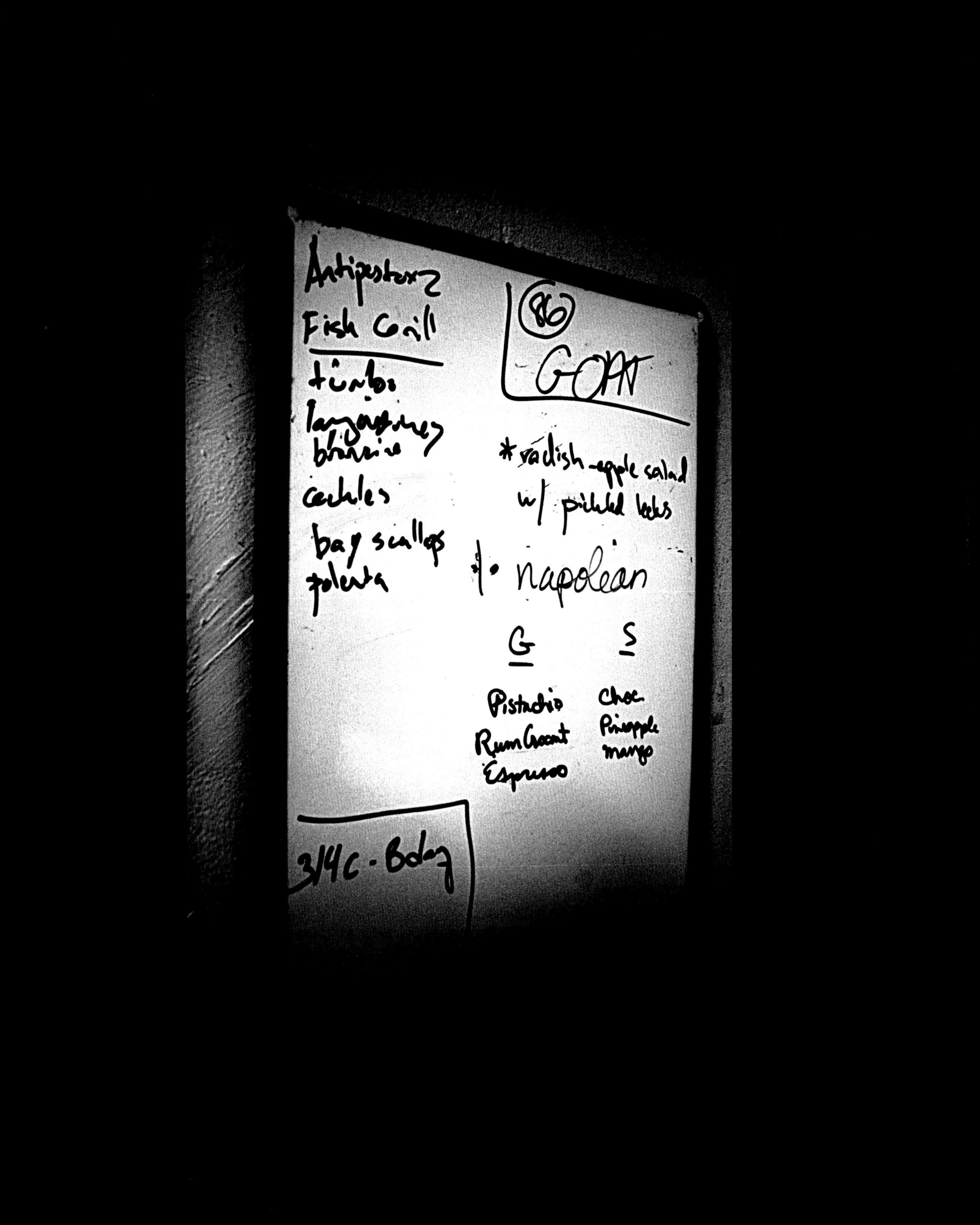

Antipasters2
Fish Grill
_____
turbo
langoustines
braavise
cochiles
bay scallops
polenta

86
GOAT
_____

* radish apple salad
  w/ pickled leeks

* napolean

G   S

Pistachio   Choc.
RumCocont   Pineapple
Espresso   mango

3/4c · Bday

4. HOT APPETIZERS
antipasti caldi

One day during prep, Paolo Frosio came into the taverna kitchen. He approached me and apologized that he didn't have room for me at his restaurant when I first arrived in Bergamo. I told him it was no problem because I was learning so much. Then Paolo asked if I wanted to work at his restaurant for a month while I was staying at the taverna apartment. Even though I had just gotten into a rhythm, I jumped at the chance. Taverna was like a culinary school, a big, opulent place with many cooks to learn from. But Frosio was that little chef-owned restaurant that everyone aspires to own. Frosio cooked his own food, did things his own way. He earned a Michelin star the second year he was open. He could teach me a lot.

I cooked on and off at Frosio for three months. Paolo opened my eyes to a precise and creative style of cooking: innovative and playful yet skilled and perfectionist. I remember how he glided effortlessly around the kitchen in his white leather clogs. I also recall how, whenever he spoke, his right eye opened wider than his left. On my first day during dinner service, Paolo stood at the plating table and another cook brought him a burnished pan filled with plump pieces of meat the size of pears. They were braised veal cheeks. Paolo lifted each cheek from the pan and placed it in a deep plate. Another smaller saucepan appeared on the table, and Paolo calmly ladled a veal reduction sauce over the cheeks. Next, he positioned a set of beautiful spears made from porcini mushroom caps and thick squares of polenta alternately threaded on branches of fresh rosemary. Paolo positioned the skewers over the top and sent the orders out.

Every one of Paolo's dishes was like this. Simple. Beautiful. Calmly plated and sent out. He was completely serene and at ease with his staff, like a maestro at a podium. He had such poise and balance that his head rarely moved as he worked, even though his hands were constantly chopping, stirring, mixing, and saucing. His mouth could be cursing a mile a minute at his brother, Camillo, but his hands would always be finishing elegant dishes and passing plates for service.

I distinctly recall the spinach flan Paolo made on my first night. He pureed blanched spinach, added an egg, a little cream, and some flour to bind it, and divided the custard among soufflé tins. Paolo then did the most amazing thing. He dropped an egg yolk into the center of each tin. When the flans were done, he called me over. I watched him unmold one of them onto a plate. He sprinkled some grated Parmesan on top and then looked at me and cut the flan from the center outward with a knife. Slowly, this gorgeous red egg yolk began oozing onto the plate. With the green spinach, the red yolk, and the white Parmesan, it was like the Italian flag. Here was world-class food that also put on a show. This was a new concept that I would always remember.

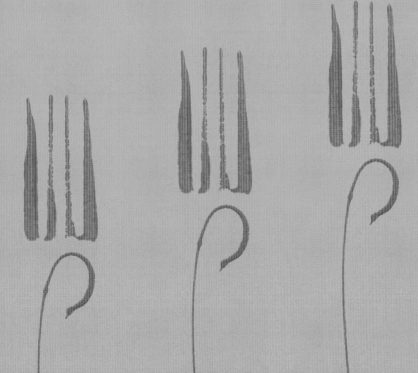

CAULIFLOWER FLAN WITH EGG YOLK 68
sformato di cavolfiore con tuorlo d'uovo

SWEET ONION CRÊPE WITH WHITE TRUFFLE FONDUE 70
crespella di cipolle dolci con fonduta al tartufo bianco

CHANTERELLE MUSHROOM CAPPUCCINO 72
cappuccino di finferli

PEACHES AND PORCINI 73
pesche e porcini

ARTICHOKE STEW WITH BUFFALO MOZZARELLA AND PISTACHIO 74
stufato di carciofi con mozzarella di bufala e pistacchio

BLUE FOOT MUSHROOMS WITH CASTELMAGNO FONDUE 76
funghi blue foot con fonduta di castelmagno

FRIED BEIGNETS WITH MORTADELLA MOUSSE 77
frittelle con spuma di mortadella

POLENTA WITH SNAILS AND PROVOLONE FONDUE 79
polenta con lumache e fonduta di provolone

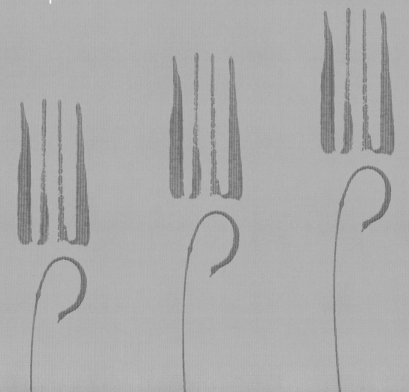

SQUID AND ARTICHOKE GALETTE 80
tortino di calamari e carciofi

BACCALÀ CREMA WITH FRIED LANGOUSTINES 82
crema di baccalà con scampi croccanti

MORTADELLA-STUFFED SQUID WITH SPRING PEAS AND PANCETTA 85
calamari farciti con mortadella, piselli di primavera e pancetta

HOMEMADE COTECHINO STUFFED WITH PICKLED VEGETABLES 86
cotechino nostrano farcito con sottaceti

VEAL KIDNEY WITH COGNAC, POLENTA, AND EGG YOLK 89
rognone di vitello con cognac, polenta e tuorlo d'uovo

TRIPE STEW 90
trippa in umido

CAULIFLOWER FLAN WITH EGG YOLK

In 2004, I spent Easter in Italy and had dinner at my friend Paolo Frosio's restaurant. Paolo sent out a spinach flan, one of his classics that he had shown me how to make years before when I worked in his kitchen. Just as before, the flan blew me away. When I got home, I started experimenting. It was springtime, so we made the flan with asparagus and put it on the menu. When autumn rolled around, I knew we couldn't continue to make it with asparagus, so we tried other vegetables. Broccoli was okay, but not great. Then, closer to winter, we made the flan with cauliflower. It was a revelation. The cauliflower pureed beautifully and echoed the whiteness of winter snow. We put in a little truffle and that, combined with the flowing egg yolk, made the dish sing. **Makes 6 servings**

12 ounces (4 cups) cauliflower florets

3 tablespoons heavy cream

1 large whole egg

1 tablespoon tipo 00 flour or all-purpose flour

Kosher salt and freshly ground black pepper

Freshly grated nutmeg

1 tablespoon unsalted butter

6 large egg yolks

1 black truffle (1/2 ounce)

6 slices pancetta

1/4 cup grated Parmesan cheese

Bring a large saucepan of salted water to a boil. Add the cauliflower and boil for about 4 minutes, or just until tender. Drain the cauliflower, transfer to a blender, and process until very smooth and thick, adding a little water if it is too thick. You should have about 1 cup of puree. Strain the puree through a fine-mesh sieve into a bowl, and gently whisk in the cream, whole egg, and flour. Season with salt, pepper, and a touch of nutmeg.

Butter six 1/2-cup soufflé cups. Fill each cup halfway full with the mixture. Gently place a raw egg yolk in the center of the mixture in each cup and top with a shaving or two of truffle. Cover with the remaining mixture, making sure the egg yolk is completely covered.

Pour water to a depth of 1/2 inch into the bottom of a wide saucepan large enough to hold the soufflé cups without touching and place over high heat. When the water boils, put the soufflé cups directly into the water (the water should come about halfway up the sides of the cups) and cover the pan. Cook for about 8 minutes, or until the mixture is set (the yolk should still be loose).

Just before the flans are ready, heat a frying pan over medium heat and fry the pancetta for 3 to 4 minutes, or until golden brown and crispy on the edges. Transfer to paper towels to drain, then cut into large bite-size pieces and keep warm.

Remove the soufflé cups from the water bath. Gently invert each cup onto a plate, to avoid breaking the yolk. The easiest way is to invert the plate over the top of the soufflé cup, gently invert the cup and plate together, and then lift off the cup, allowing the flan to slide free.

Sprinkle each flan with a little of the Parmesan. Cut the pancetta slices into pieces and top the flans with the pieces.

PREP AHEAD

You can make the custard mixture up to 1 day ahead and keep it, tightly covered, in the refrigerator.

IMPROV

To serve the flan in the springtime, use asparagus instead of cauliflower. The proportions are slightly different because asparagus has a less creamy texture than cauliflower. Use 1 bunch asparagus (enough to make 1 cup puree), 1/4 cup heavy cream, 2 large eggs, and 2 tablespoons flour. Make 1 1/4 cups White Truffle Fondue (page 276) and spoon around the flan just before serving.

VINO ·

This dish is rich and delicate at the same time, and the wine should perform a similar balancing act. Schiopetto Pinot Bianco from Friuli is my favorite pairing. It has a touch of smokiness that accentuates the black truffle and just enough crispness to let the creamy flan glide across the palate. For something a little more off the beaten path, look for Sauvignon Blanc from Ignaz Niedrist, in Alto Adige. His wines tend toward the earthier Alsatian style, a characteristic that elevates the truffle flavor. —J.B.

SWEET ONION CRÊPE WITH WHITE TRUFFLE FONDUE

We used to make this dish by cooking fifty pounds of sliced onions for two to three hours, and then whisking in some toasted flour to thicken them up. But I wanted the color of the onions to be darker, so we started letting them cook longer and longer until they were deeply browned. The long cooking also made the onions taste sweeter, more like onion marmalade, which proved the perfect complement to the cream and truffle. Now we let the onions cook all day— seven to eight hours—over the lowest possible heat. **Makes 6 servings**

SWEET ONION FILLING

3 large onions

1 tablespoon unsalted butter

1 teaspoon extra virgin olive oil

Kosher salt

CRÊPES

1/2 cup tipo 00 flour or all-purpose flour

1/2 cup whole milk

1 large egg

1 tablespoon grape seed oil

Kosher salt and freshly ground black pepper

Freshly grated nutmeg

Grated Parmesan cheese

1 1/4 cups White Truffle Fondue (page 276)

For the sweet onion filling: Cut the onions in half and thinly slice them. Put the onions in a large cold pan with the butter, olive oil, and a pinch of salt. Place over the lowest possible heat and cook for 2 to 2½ hours, stirring occasionally to avoid sticking and burning. The onions should be deep brown. If they are pale or you can't wait, increase the heat to medium and cook until deeply browned. Spread out the onions in a single layer on a sheet pan and let cool.

For the crêpes: In a bowl, whisk together the flour, milk, eggs, and grape seed oil until very smooth. Season lightly with salt and pepper and a touch of nutmeg. Place a 10-inch nonstick pan (preferably square) or nonstick crêpe pan over low heat. When hot, ladle in enough batter to cover the bottom of the pan in a thin layer. Cook the crêpe for about 1 minute, or until you can flip it over without breaking it. Flip and cook for another 30 seconds. Remove the crêpe from the pan and let cool. Repeat with the remaining batter, letting the crêpes cool in a single layer. You should have about 4 crêpes.

Preheat the oven to 500°F. When the crêpes and onions are completely cool, lay a crêpe on a work surface. Spread about ⅓ cup of the onion mixture evenly over the surface. Roll up the crêpe and cut crosswise into slices about ½ inch to 1 inch thick. Arrange the slices, with a cut side down, on a sheet pan. Repeat with the remaining crêpes and onion mixture. Lightly sprinkle the slices with Parmesan. Bake for 5 to 6 minutes, or until crispy.

Meanwhile, make the fondue and keep warm.

To finish: Spoon a pool of fondue onto each plate and place a crispy crêpe slice on top (as shown in the photo). To serve a more substantial appetizer, serve slices on each plate.

PREP AHEAD

The crêpes and the onion filling can be prepared and refrigerated separately, well covered, for up to 1 day before assembling and cooking.

VINO ·

With sweet onions and sweet cream, this dish screams for acid. Picture candied lemon-peel jellies dusted with sugar: that's the interplay of acidity and sweetness you are looking for. But be careful because the truffle fondue needs some earthiness, too. Diego Bolognani's Müller-Thurgau (a hybrid grape that crosses Riesling and Sylvaner), from the alpine slopes of Trentino, strikes that balance. The bone-dry Riesling provides the acid, and the grassiness of Sylvaner complements the fondue. —J.B.

CHANTERELLE MUSHROOM CAPPUCCINO

In 2003, we added a restored 1958 Faema Urania espresso machine to the dining room. As soon as it arrived, I wanted to play with it every day. We used the machine's steamer for everything: fish, vegetables . . . you name it. One fall day, we made a chanterelle mushroom soup that we ladled into coffee cups for serving. We left the cups sitting on the counter next to the coffee machine. At a quick glance, they appeared to be filled with espresso. I foamed some milk and spooned it over the soup. It made total sense. And still does.

Makes 6 servings

> 2 tablespoons unsalted butter
>
> 1 pound chanterelle mushrooms, brushed clean and thinly sliced
>
> 1/4 cup olive oil
>
> 2 thyme sprigs
>
> 1 onion, coarsely chopped
>
> 1 clove garlic, finely chopped
>
> 2 tablespoons sherry vinegar
>
> 3 cups Chicken Stock (page 274)
>
> Kosher salt and freshly ground black pepper
>
> 1 cup whole milk
>
> Freshly grated nutmeg

Melt 1 tablespoon of the butter in a saucepan over medium-high heat. When it foams, add the mushrooms and sauté for about 3 minutes, or until they begin to wilt. Remove from the pan and keep warm. Reserve about 18 slices for garnish.

Put 1 tablespoon of the oil and the remaining 1 tablespoon butter in the pan over medium-high heat. When hot, add the thyme and onion and stir for about 1 minute, until the onion begins to release moisture. Return the mushrooms to the pan, add the garlic, and cook for about 3 minutes, or until the onion is translucent but not brown. Add 1 tablespoon of the vinegar. When the vinegar begins to sizzle, add the stock. Bring to a boil over high heat, reduce the heat to low, and cook for about 5 minutes, or until the mushrooms are tender.

Remove the thyme sprigs and pour the entire mixture into a blender or food processor. Engage the motor and then carefully remove the cover or open the feed tube and drizzle in 2 teaspoons of the remaining vinegar and the remaining 3 tablespoons olive oil, processing until smooth. Season lightly with salt and pepper.

Put the milk, the remaining 1 teaspoon vinegar, and a pinch of salt in a cappuccino frother and foam the mixture. Or, if you have no frother, put the milk, vinegar, and salt in a small saucepan, bring to a boil over medium heat, and boil just until it starts to boil over. Remove from the heat and you will have the foam you need to finish the dish.

Pour the soup into warmed oversized cappuccino cups and top with the foam. Grate some nutmeg lightly on top, and garnish each cup with 3 of the reserved mushroom slices.

IMPROV

You can experiment with other mushrooms here, but I recommend sticking with the more delicate varieties, such as hedgehog, a type of chanterelle. For herbs, you can use marjoram instead of thyme. Both are members of the mint family. Thyme lends a subtle lemonlike aroma, while marjoram gives the soup a little sweetness reminiscent of oregano.

VINO ··

A sparkling wine is called for here. I tend to favor a nonvintage brut from Ca' del Bosco, from the Franciacorta wine region, which lies west of Brescia in Lombardy. Its somewhat yeasty finish and effervescence play well with the earthiness and foam in the dish. If you are more adventuresome, try Deus Brut des Flandres, an amazing Belgian beer. After the normal fermentation, it is bottled and shipped to Champagne, where fermentable sugar and yeast are added, and from there it is treated much like Champagne—riddled and all—for twelve months. It has a creamy texture and lower alcohol content, yet retains the yeasty complement. —J.B.

PEACHES AND PORCINI

People are often amazed when they nibble this appetizer, thinking they have discovered the best flavor combination ever. And they are sometimes surprised to hear it is a classic pairing in northern Italy. Meaty, earthy-tasting porcini mushrooms work well with almost any fruit, especially musky peaches. If you like the combination, taste a similar pairing in Porcini and Blueberry Lasagna (page 139). **Makes 4 servings**

2 ripe yet firm peaches

2 tablespoons extra virgin olive oil

2 tablespoons unsalted butter

8 ounces chopped porcini mushrooms

2 tablespoons chopped onion

2 cups Chicken Stock (page 274)

6 drops sherry vinegar

2 teaspoons heavy cream

2 teaspoons chopped fresh flat-leaf parsley

Kosher salt and freshly ground black pepper

Peel, halve, and pit the peaches and cut into 1/8-inch-thick slices.

Heat the oil and butter in a sauté pan over high heat. When the butter foams, add the peaches, mushrooms, and onion and cook, stirring occasionally, for 3 to 4 minutes, or until glossy. Add the stock, vinegar, and cream and boil for 1 to 2 minutes, or until reduced by about half.

Stir in the parsley and season with salt and pepper. Serve on warmed plates.

VINO ·

Look for an unoaked white with a tart, minerally profile. Librandi's vibrant Critone from Calabria, a blend of 90 percent Chardonnay and 10 percent Sauvignon Blanc, has a crisp, clean mouthfeel that lets the mushrooms and peaches speak for themselves. —J.B.

ARTICHOKE STEW WITH BUFFALO MOZZARELLA AND PISTACHIO

California grows most of the artichoke crop in the United States, but Italy is the largest producer of artichokes in the world. In Italian markets, you see dozens of different varieties. Baby artichokes are my favorite. They are not really immature artichokes, just smaller ones that grow farther down the plant. They are much easier to eat than larger varieties because the fuzzy choke isn't fully developed. Trim off the outer green leaves, cut the baby artichokes in half lengthwise, and then cook them however you like. I like to simmer them with pancetta and mirepoix, and top them off with buffalo mozzarella and toasted pistachios. **Makes 4 to 6 servings**

> 2 tablespoons pistachio nuts, preferably Sicilian
> 4 cups water
> 1 tablespoon fresh lemon juice
> 10 baby artichokes (about 2 pounds total)
> 1/4 cup olive oil
> 1 small carrot, peeled and diced
> 1/2 onion, diced
> 1 celery stalk, diced
> 2 ounces pancetta, finely chopped
> Kosher salt and freshly ground black pepper
> 1 cup dry white wine
> 2 cups Chicken Stock (page 274)
> 1/2 cup grated Parmesan cheese
> 10 ounces buffalo mozzarella cheese, sliced
> 10 fresh basil leaves, minced

Put the pistachios in a large sauté pan over medium heat. Toast, shaking the pan every now and again, for about 4 minutes, or until the pistachios are fragrant. Remove from the pan, let cool, and then chop.

Fill a stainless-steel or other nonreactive bowl with the water and add the lemon juice. Working with 1 artichoke at a time, snap off the tough outer green leaves until you are left with a small bullet-shaped artichoke with pale yellow leaves that turn green just at the tips. Cut off the green tips crosswise. Cut the stem flush with the bottom of the artichoke so that no green remains, cut the artichoke in half lengthwise, and scoop out and discard any choke. Immediately toss the halves into the lemon water to inhibit browning.

Return the sauté pan to medium-high heat and add 2 tablespoons of the oil to the pan. Add the carrot, onion, celery, and pancetta and sauté for about 5 minutes, or until the vegetables begin to soften. Season with salt and pepper. Drain the artichokes, add to the pan, and cook for 1 minute. Pour in the wine and cook for about 5 minutes, or until the liquid has reduced by half. Add the stock and cook for another 5 minutes or so, or until the artichokes are tender.

Transfer 1 cup of the liquid (bits of vegetable are okay) and 2 artichoke halves to a blender and process until smooth. Return the puree to the stew along with the Parmesan and stir to combine.

Spoon the artichokes and some of their cooking liquid onto a platter or individual plates. Top with the mozzarella and basil, and drizzle with the remaining 2 tablespoons oil. Sprinkle with the pistachios and a fresh grinding of pepper.

PREP AHEAD
When chopping the vegetables for this dish, prepare the baby artichokes last to minimize browning. They can remain in the lemon water for up to 2 hours.

VINO ·

Artichokes contain the compound cynarine, which stimulates the sweetness receptors on your tongue so that other foods taste sweeter. To offset this effect, you need to pick a wine on the dry side. But the creaminess of the mozzarella and the nuttiness of the pistachios change our needs slightly. The wine I enjoy most with this dish is Campania Fiano di Avellino, which is dry yet velvety on the palate. Feudi di San Gregorio is one of the best and most accessible. For something different, try Franziskaner's Hefeweisse, a light-bodied wheat beer with a creamy texture that complements the silky cheese. —J.B.